580
S5

LIBRARY
CORBY HALL

Higher Learning
&
Catholic Traditions

Erasmus Institute
Books

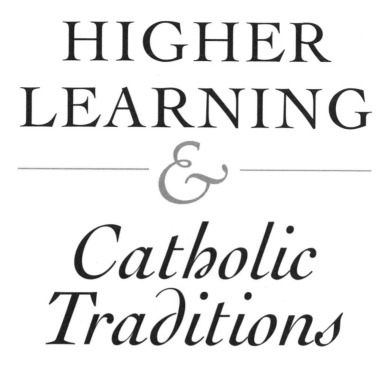

HIGHER LEARNING

LEARNING

&

Catholic Traditions

edited by

ROBERT E. SULLIVAN

University of Notre Dame Press

Notre Dame, Indiana

Copyright 2001 by
University of Notre Dame
Notre Dame, Indiana 46556
http://www.undpress.nd.edu
All Rights Reserved

Manufactured in the United States of America

Library of Congress Cataloging-in-Publication Data

Higher learning and Catholic traditions / edited by Robert E. Sullivan.
    p.   cm.
    "Erasmus Institute books."
    Includes bibliographical references and index.
    ISBN 0-268-03053-7
    1. Catholic universities and colleges.   2. Catholic learning and
scholarship.   I. Sullivan, Robert E.   II. Erasmus Institute.
  LC487.H55   2001
    378'.071273—dc21   00-011594

∞ *This book was printed on acid-free paper.*

Contents

Preface

THE MODERN INTELLECTUAL IMPACT OF CATHOLICISM, THE REST
of Christianity, and the other Abrahamic religions is discussed perhaps
more widely than credibly. There are clear and various gaps in our knowledge of how ideas inspired by Christianity have related to scholarship and
the sciences during the last three hundred years. Although a credible history of those relations is neither written nor yet writable, their character
is important to the ways contemporary believers and unbelievers understand themselves and each other. For want of anything better, a nineteenth-
century theory still informs most discussions of the modern intellectual
impact of Christianity. The earliest versions depicted the March of Mind
overriding religious dogmatism, or credulity. With the eclipse of the practice of dignifying an arguable notion by capitalizing it, that movement was
generally called "secularization." A protean concept, "secularization"
expanded only in the 1860s from a legal term for either the confiscation
and transfer of ecclesiastical property or the change in status of certain
ecclesiastical persons to a metaphor for the increasing cultural diminu-
tion of Christianity during modern times. Whether the movement was
depicted in roseate hues of progress or in twilight shades of decline, the
common assumption was that Catholicism and the rest of Christianity
were being intellectually isolated or excluded.

Two American polemics from a century ago, Andrew Dickson White's
A History of the Warfare of Science with Theology in Christendom and James J.
Walsh's *The Thirteenth, Greatest of Centuries*, framed the issue in recog-
nizable ways. White and Walsh contested historical details and general
evaluation, but they agreed that the connection between modern thought

and the intellectual traditions of the churches, above all of Roman Catholicism, was at best uneasy. Both White, a historian and the founding president of Cornell, and his younger contemporary Walsh, a pathologist and sometime dean of the medical school of Fordham, underwent the rite of passage common among aspiring American academics during the nineteenth century: they briefly studied at the University of Berlin, the very model of the modern major university.

First in Germany and later in the United States, the research university became the primary institution for generating the progressively expanding and specialized forms of research that now define knowledge.[1] By 1900 the dominant idea of a university was less that of an institution where students learned a body of inherited and basically fixed truths than of one that supported original research conducted within differentiated and increasingly self-contained academic disciplines and subdisciplines. Because of the manifest success and resulting prestige of the work of those who in 1833 were first called "scientists," knowledge was redefined and increasingly fragmented. As the nineteenth century unfolded, the most creative and respected scholars, imitating the example of their scientific colleagues, learned to regard as secondary both the intellectual assumptions and any wider implications of their researches, which became increasingly more specialized. Those scholars, moreover, aspired to conduct their researches according to a naturalistic method.

On that principle, a field was properly an object of academic inquiry if it admitted the collection of data that were susceptible to an inductive investigation and explanation, at best one that yielded a scientific law. The academic use of religious ideas was improper insofar as they presupposed or asserted the existence of the divine. Religious ideas could be studied as historical or sociological phenomena, but no credence could be given to their allegedly supernatural implications, which were at best metaphors for social relations and at worst residues of a thoroughly prelogical state of mind.[2] In English, the resonance of that methodological naturalism was eventually captured by *agnostic* and *agnosticism*, neologisms suggested in 1869 by T. H. Huxley, the most redoubtable champion of Charles Darwin's principle of natural selection.

Also in 1869 White aired the argument of the polemical history he finally published a generation later. A politician, diplomat, and administrator, he artfully expressed the necessary monopoly of methodological naturalism within the university. Only the laicization of academic institutions and the instruction and research they supported enabled the intellectual emancipation from "theological control" necessary for the progress of knowledge, what White called "Science."[3] A lifelong churchgoer and close auditor of sermons, he championed the flourishing of religion in its proper sphere, which was fundamentally moral and personal rather than cognitive and institutional.[4] It followed that the researches of "sober minded scholars" always regulated the limited intellectual content religion validly possessed. Anything more cognitively ambitious was "theology," in essence obscurantist and repressive speculation, a ghost of the primitive dogmatic casus belli: "More and more the thinking and controlling races are developing the power of right reason; and more and more they are leaving to the inferior and disappearing races the methods of theological dogmatism. More and more, in all parts of the civilized world, is developing liberty of thought; and more and more is left behind the tyranny of formulas."[5]

Along with thousands in America and elsewhere before and since, White accepted as self-evident a practical, inclusive philosophical method, which led its followers to deny, in Alexis de Tocqueville's words, "what they cannot comprehend; . . . [leaving] them but little faith for whatever is extraordinary and an almost insurmountable distaste for whatever is supernatural."[6] Perhaps as much as the disciplinary structure of the modern research university, the prevalence of moralistic notions of religion made it seem inconceivable that Christian intellectual traditions could somehow nourish, stimulate, or inform the advance of scholarship and science.

Walsh, in contrast, portrayed the relations between Catholic ideas and modern learning as uneasy but thought the situation was merely recent and contingent. As much as White, he avoided nuances and discriminations. In the high Middle Ages where White saw unrelieved bleakness and essential otherness, Walsh saw shafts of light pointing forward. Walsh overreached himself by insisting on the permanent importance not only of much medieval learning, but also of the usually papally-chartered universities that supported it. Those institutions formed, he insisted, "the mold in which the human intellect has been cast" ever since.[7] The originality of the modern identification of knowledge with the results of disciplinary research and its freedom from ecclesiastical supervision and, supposedly, Christian intellectual traditions baffled Walsh's cheery apologetics. The University of Berlin, where he studied with the formidable pathologist Rudolf Virchow, who first described the battle against institutional Catholicism in which he soldiered under Otto von Bismarck during the 1870s as "Kulturkampf," was fundamentally different from the University of Paris when Thomas Aquinas expounded theology. The disciplinary, naturalistic pursuit of knowledge separated the modern university from its medieval antecedents.

Twentieth-century Roman Catholic universities and colleges offered little resistance to the secularization of the idea of knowledge. The Scholastic philosophy that was dominant during much of their twentieth-century history was meant to serve "as the linchpin of curricular integration," but it was in its own way highly rationalistic and effectively secularizing.[8] Divorced from theology, it assumed that a sharp division between the "natural" and the "supernatural" yielded a spacious domain of pure nature (*natura pura*) governed by unaided human reason. In practice, that assumption apparently meant that most Catholic institutions imposed on their undergraduates a heavy load of prescribed courses in Scholastic philosophy that were largely unconnected with what they learned in the departments where they majored or in the professional schools where they enrolled. There, knowledge was increasingly organized and divided in the conventional way, according to specialized academic disciplines that more or less conformed to the conventional standards of methodological naturalism. In the Catholic academic milieu fifty years ago, "integration" seemingly possessed something of the Grail-like allure and elusiveness that would later mark numerous interdisciplinary projects.

The study of Catholic and other Christian and monotheistic intellectual traditions is still routinely confined to seminaries, divinity schools, and departments of theology or religious studies, which often seem cut off from the wider academic world. It is easy to ignore the possibility that those traditions have implications for the advancement of "secular" knowledge. Informed by greater learning and subtlety and free of racism, something like Andrew Dickson White's point of view about religion and higher learning often prevails.[9] True religion is basically about ethics, or values, rather than knowledge. The relations between modern disciplinary knowledge and the intellectual traditions of Catholicism and other forms of Christianity are necessarily uneasy, if not quite inimical. As a result, the modernity and eminence of any university is judged in large measure by the success of its adaptation to the methodological naturalism of the disciplines. It is telling that the most sophisticated history of Catholic higher education in America is entitled *Contending with Modernity*.

The Erasmus Institute was founded in 1997 through the generosity of an anonymous donor, The Pew Charitable Trusts, and the University of

Notre Dame to try to build bridges between the apparently disconnected worlds of Catholic thought and secular scholarship.[10] The institute encourages the application of Catholic intellectual traditions to research outside of academic theology in the disciplines of the humanities and social sciences, including the arts and professional fields such as law. It also supports parallel work grounded in the intellectual traditions of other Christian faiths, of Judaism, and of Islam. A competitive, nonsectarian fellowship program annually brings at least nine fellows to the institute, which is centered at Notre Dame, normally for a year of concentrated research and writing on projects related to the institute's goals. The fellows range from distinguished senior scholars to dissertation writers, and they carry out their work in the atmosphere of a mutually supporting intellectual community. In addition, the institute seeks through summer programs, which take place annually on the campus of a different university or college, to nurture a new generation of scholars interested in research grounded in Catholic intellectual traditions. Like the residential fellows, the participants in the summer programs are selected through a competitive national application process. The institute also sponsors small working-groups of scholars pursuing related or collaborative projects, programs on the Notre Dame campus, and academic conferences both in the United States and abroad.

The essays in this volume, which inaugurates the Erasmus Institute Books series, began life as papers delivered at a conference entitled "Higher Learning and Catholic Traditions," held at the University of Notre Dame on 13–14 October 1999. Distinguished academics from a variety of intellectual and religious backgrounds were asked to explore from the perspectives of their own disciplinary competence possible new relationships between Catholic intellectual traditions and the dominant secular culture of higher education. Jean Bethke Elshtain's helpful overview of their essays establishes some points of both convergence and dispute among the essays. A preview is unnecessary.

Some of the essays, however, may be read as subverting the received story of the modern sundering of the worlds of secular scholarship and Catholic thought. Alan Wolfe, for example, knows that "there is . . . no one sociological tradition against which Catholicism can be contrasted." He also sketches a history of the origin of sociology that centers on Emile Durkheim and Max Weber as thinkers of primarily secular inspiration.[11] An alternative history may better explain why the later British Catholic social scientists Edward Evans-Pritchard, Victor Turner, and Mary Douglas found in the Durkheimian school the intellectual resources they needed to pursue their fruitful and influential researches into ritual and symbol, expressions and sources of sociability which were for them religiously congenial.[12] On that interpretation, the theoretical orientation informing their vigorously empirical fieldwork originated in the anti-individualist theological and political polemics of reactionary nineteenth-century French Catholic thinkers like Louis de Bonald.[13] A line runs from some of their organicist ideas via those of the Comte de Saint-Simon to those of Durkheim and beyond. On that interpretation, the twentieth-century Anglophone history of Durkheim's school may be plausibly read at least as much as one of renovation or recovery as of innovative assimilation.

In a similar way, Bruce Russett's project of updating Immanuel Kant's *On Perpetual Peace* (*Zum ewigen Frieden*, 1795) by giving it a solid empirical foundation ends with the cautious suggestion that the Kantian project of international relations is "not alien to the Catholic tradition, recent or ancient." Professor Russett properly shows certain affinities between the Kantian vision and recent official Catholic teachings on peace. Worth mentioning is the kinship between Kant's project and the political ideas of some earlier Catholic thinkers. Kant's view of human rights developed the insights not only of the Protestant philosophers Samuel Pufendorf and Hugo Grotius but also of the baroque Jesuit Scholastic theologian Francisco Suarez.[14] Kant wrote, moreover, from within a European anti-Machiavellian tradition of ideas about statecraft that included a vigorous Catholic wing.[15]

Russett's essay, along with those of several other contributors, suggests a possibly illuminating but still barely explored area: the impact of philosophical idealism, perhaps the most enduring intellectual style within modern German universities, on disparate Catholic thinkers. Its considerable early-nineteenth-century vogue among some Catholics has long been known, but the revival of neo-Thomism, particularly after 1878 when Pope Leo XIII mandated it for the entire church, is often taken as inaugurating a caesura.[16] If only because of the ancient, weighty debt of Christian thought to forms of Platonism, various interactions between Catholicism and idealism continued, despite the often loud controversies between the Neo-Thomists and the Neo-Kantians as well as other idealist philosophers. There are probably many precursors of the contemporary theologian Hans Urs von Balthasar's unacknowledged borrowing from German philosophical idealism, which Nicholas Boyle describes in his essay. The twentieth-century Catholic effort to reconcile Thomism and Kantianism, often described as transcendental Thomism, debuted as early as 1908, and the effort may prove to be the explicit culmination of a long-standing, largely unspoken, intellectual symbiosis.[17] The separation between some central aspects of modern thought and various Catholic intellectual traditions was probably less complete than champions of methodological naturalism, and not a few of their Catholic critics, chose to imagine. Considering some limitations of the metaphors of *warfare* and *secularization* as explanations of the past relationships between higher learning and Catholic intellectual traditions is merely a prefatory ground-clearing. Far more important for the future are the present hopeful tokens of the expansion of those relations.

In editing these essays, I enjoyed the competent and cheerful assistance of Rebecca DeBoer, Andy McBride, Terri O'Reilly, and Kathy Sobieralski, whom I gratefully acknowledge.

Robert E. Sullivan

NOTES

1. Laurence R. Veysey, *The Emergence of the American University* (Chicago: University of Chicago Press, 1965), remains the starting point for understanding the American side of that history; it is most recently traced in Jon H. Roberts and James Turner, *The Sacred and the Secular University* (Princeton: Princeton University Press, 2000), with detailed references; glimpses of the international context are offered in Sheldon Rothblatt and Björn Wittrock, eds., *The European and American University since 1800* (Cambridge and New York: Cambridge University Press, 1993).

2. A classic expression of the contrast between an attentive if reductionist notion of the cognitive status of religious ideas and a notion of them that is dichotomous and essentially dismissive is found in Emile Durkheim, review of *Les fonctions mentales dans les sociétés inférieures*, by Lucien Lévy-Bruhl, and of *Les formes élémentaires de la vie religieuse*, by Emile Durkheim, *L'Année sociologique* 12 (1909–12): 33–37.

3. Andrew Dickson White, *A History of the Warfare of Science with Theology in Christendom*, 2 vols. (New York, 1896), 1:xi–xii, 414–15.

4. For his churchgoing, see *The Diaries of Andrew D. White*, ed. Robert Morris Ogden (Ithaca, N.Y.: Cornell University Library, 1959), 116, 125, 131, 150, 155, 191, 220, 273, 275, 277, 397, 399, 402–3, 408, 419, 433, 451, 466, 482, etc.; for the evolution of his religious opinions, "Religious Development," part 8 in *Autobiography of Andrew Dickson White*, 2 vols. (New York: Century Co., 1905).

5. White, *Autobiography*, 2:571.

6. Alexis de Tocqueville, *Democracy in America*, trans. Henry Reeve, ed. Phillips Bradley, 2 vols. (New York: Vintage Books, 1956), 2:4; the entire first section of that volume, "Influence of Democracy on the Action of Intellect in the United States," is now more widely pertinent.

7. James J. Walsh, *The Thirteenth, Greatest of Centuries* (New York: Catholic Summer School Press, 1907), 18–19; cf. vi, 32, 78–79.

8. Philip Gleason, *Contending with Modernity: Catholic Higher Education in the Twentieth Century* (New York and Oxford: Oxford University Press, 1995), 164.

9. E.g., Martha C. Nussbaum, "Socrates in the Religious University," chap. 8 in *Cultivating Humanity: A Classical Defense of Reform in Liberal Education* (Cambridge, Mass.: Harvard University Press, 1997).

10. James Turner, "Catholic Intellectual Traditions and Contemporary Scholarship" (Notre Dame, Ind.: Charles and Margaret Hall Cushwa Center for the Study of American Catholicism, 1997), offers a programmatic statement for the Erasmus Institute.

11. Raymond Aron, *Les étapes de la pensée sociologique* (Paris: Gallimard, 1967).

12. Richard Fardon, *Mary Douglas: An Intellectual Biography* (London and New York: Routledge, 1999), captures aspects of that development.

13. That version is traced in Robert A. Nisbet, *The Sociological Tradition* (New York: Basic Books, 1966), and Tom Bottomore and Robert Nisbet, eds., *A History of Sociological Analysis* (New York: Basic Books, 1978); Mary Pickering, *Auguste Comte: An Intellectual Biography*, vol.1 (Cambridge: Cambridge University Press, 1993), captures in a masterly fashion that Catholic intellectual milieu.

14. Peter Huggenmacher, "Kant et la tradition du droit des gens," in *L'Année 1795: Kant, Essai sur la paix*, ed. Pierre Laberge, Guy Lafrance, and Denis Demas (Paris: J. Vrin, 1997), 122–39.

15. Cf. Reinhard Brandt, "Historisch-kritische Beobachtungen zu Kants Friedensschrift," in *"Zur ewigen Frieden": Grundlagen, Aktualität und Aussichten einer Idee von Immanuel Kant*, ed. Reinhard Merkel and Roland Wittmann (Frankfurt am Main: Suhrkamp, 1996), 31–66, particularly 63–64, and Robert Bireley, *The Counter-Reformation Prince: Anti-Machiavellianism or Catholic Statecraft in Early Modern Europe* (Chapel Hill: University of North Carolina Press, 1990), 216–42.

16. E.g., Henri Gouhier, *Les conversions de Maine de Biran: Histoire philosophique du sentiment religieux en France* (Paris: J. Vrin, 1947), Joseph Rupert Geiselmann, *Geist des Christentums und des Katholizismus: Ausgewählte Schriften katholischer Theologie im Zeitalter des deutschen Idealismus und der Romantik* (Mainz: Matthias-Grunewald-Verlag, 1940), and *Die katholische Tübinger Schule* (Freiburg: Herder, 1964).

17. Pierre Rousselot, S.J., *L'Intellectualisme de S. Thomas* (Paris: Beauchesne, 1908).

1

Catholic Universities

Dangers, Hopes, Choices

ALASDAIR MACINTYRE

1. The Integrative Tasks of a Catholic University

It is sometimes thought to be obvious that what Catholics and secularizing unbelievers disagree about in respect of colleges and universities is no more than a matter of the place that explicitly religious belief and practice should have in collegiate and university life. But this is a mistake, one that may prevent us from learning what some of the most insightful Catholic writers about universities have to teach us, namely that universities which become what the great American research universities of the present have become may be judged to have failed, not because they are not Catholic or otherwise Christian, but because they are in grave danger of no longer functioning as universities. How so?

A thesis recurrently asserted in Catholic writing about universities from Newman's 1852 discourses to John Paul II's 1989 allocution concerns the secondary, even if essential, place of the specialized academic disciplines in university education. That research within those disciplines is a good is never denied. That students need instruction in such specialized branches of knowledge is always affirmed. But that research and that instruction have a due place in universities only insofar as they also serve a further end, that of contributing to and finding their place within an integrated understanding of the order of things.

Newman argued not only that the end of university education is excellence and enlargement of mind, but that these cannot be achieved either by intensive training within one academic discipline or even within a number of such disciplines. "That only is true enlargement of mind," he wrote, "which is the power of viewing many things at once as one whole, of referring them severally to their true place in the universal system, of understanding their respective values, and determining their mutual dependence. . . . Possessed of this real illumination, the mind never views any part of the extended subject-matter of Knowledge without recollecting that it is but a part."[1] This enlargement of the mind constitutes, Newman says, the perfection of intellect. It finds expression in a capacity for judgment that cannot be acquired from the specialized disciplines alone.

Similarly, John Paul II has portrayed Catholic universities as places where not only is "each individual discipline studied in a systematic manner," but where "scholars will be engaged in a constant effort to determine the relative place and meaning of each of the various disciplines within the context of a vision of the human person and the world."[2] In Catholic universities this integrative task is understood as having an essential theological dimension. But the integrative task is nonetheless a task for secular reason and a task for the secular university and to abandon it is to endanger the functioning of universities as universities, rather than as mere assemblages of assorted disciplinary enterprises.

We need, then, to understand this integrative task better. Its aim is to transform the mind of the student, or rather to work with the student toward her or his self-transformation, so that students become able to exercise a full range of powers of understanding and judgment. What are the marks of a mind thus educated? First, students must have learned to recognize when they do not understand and what they do not understand. Our students need, *we* need, to learn to be constantly surprised, astonished, and perplexed. And it is a great defect in too many of our students and in ourselves that they and we do not find enough of the world astonishing or puzzling, and one reason why they and we do not is that they and we too often think of all problems as puzzles internal to and to be solved by means of the enquiries of the specialized disciplines. What in consequence they and we fail to be sufficiently perplexed by is how to bring to bear the findings of those disciplines on questions that cannot be answered in this way.

Secondly, therefore, it is the mark of a mind thus educated, when confronted by perplexity, to know how to bring the various findings and methods of different specialized disciplines to bear on that perplexity. And this of course cannot be achieved without depth of knowledge in some at least of the specialized disciplines. But knowing how to bring to bear the findings or methods of this or that specialized discipline on the tasks of understanding is not something that can be learned from those disciplines themselves. An education whose end products are no more than superbly trained specialists, each of whom has learned to focus narrowly on this or that area, provides only a distorted and one-sided development of the mind. We always need to remind ourselves of something that experience on university committees irritatingly often confirms, that it is possible to have become a highly distinguished historian, say, or physicist and yet remain a fool.

An educated mind, then, knows how to be perplexed and is excited by perplexity into summoning up resources from the relevant specialized disciplines. It does so in the interests of arriving not only at the truth about this or that particular subject-matter, but at that truth the attainment of which constitutes completed understanding, the adequacy of mind to its objects, a grasp of objects that may bring into relationship any number of dimensions. We need first to understand what the object that perplexes us *is*: an earthquake with expectation-defying patterns of devastation; a hybrid rose with unusual properties; the unpredicted outcome of a tank battle; the text of a poem open to alternative interpretations. And the tasks of understanding will initially take us in more than one direction: to geological explanations of the genesis of the earthquake and to architectural and social historians' explanations of the types of building that were or were not destroyed; to the plant geneticist's work on hybrid roses, to the historian's study of rose-growing, and to the economist's of the relevant markets; to metallurgists', engineers', and military historians' contributions to the understanding of why the tank battle went as it did; to the bearing on the interpretation of this particular poem of issues of translation and genre and their relationship to the social role of poets in that particular culture.

Yet each of these contributions has to be put to the service of answering still further questions, if the tasks of understanding are to be completed: What does *this* poem achieve that no other poem has achieved and how does it achieve it? What were the goods at stake in the outcome of this battle and what goods or evils issued from it? What did the culture of this type of rose contribute to human flourishing? What different parts do earthquakes play in the history of our planet as plant, animal, and human habitat?

Adequate answers to these latter questions assist in moving toward a completed understanding of whatever it was that first puzzled us by situating it in the context of those relationships that define its place in the order of things. For the presupposition of this way of understanding the project of understanding is that there is an order of things, that the natural and human world are so structured that the properties of what is found at each level of that structured order make possible and place constraints upon what kinds of things there are and what occurs at higher levels. Subatomic particles make molecules possible and impose constraints upon them, and so too with the relationships of molecules to cells, of cells to plants and animals, and of all of these to human beings in their social relationships. To understand some particular phenomenon is to know of it how it came to be and what sustains it in being, and if it is a plant or an animal, what it is for it to flourish and what has fostered or prevented its flourishing, and, if it is a human being or a human society, what features of its particular social and cultural order have enabled it to flourish or caused it to fail to flourish. This is a universe, on this view of it, that is at once Catholic and secular, in which purpose is at home, in which human and other goods are integral to the intelligible order of things, and in which the project of making that order of things intelligible to us through the activities of enquiry proper to universities is itself to be understood as a part of the order of things. The questions of what purposes the activities of universities serve and of what goods are at stake in our succeeding or failing in those activities are just the kinds of questions that it is the purpose of universities to pursue. And, as with other such questions, although we may learn much that is relevant from specialized disciplines, about, for example, the history, economics, and anthropology of universities, we shall find no adequate answer from within such disciplines.

It is of course Catholic dogmatic teaching that the natural order of things is adequately understood by reason only when understood as brought into being by God and as directed toward the ends to which He orders it. But what is learned from nature about God and His ordering of the created universe is at best meager and in practice always liable to and generally subject to distortions deriving from human limitations and human sin. Universities always need, therefore, both the enlargement of vision and the correction of error that can be provided only from a theological standpoint, one that brings truths of Christian revelation to bear on our studies. So our integrative tasks are of two kinds. One set can be carried out only by rational enquiry, independently of faith and revealed truths, enabling enquirers to understand how the specialized disciplines contribute to, but cannot themselves supply, an understanding of the overall order of things. These are the tasks of philosophy, rightly understood. And there is a second set of tasks that can be carried out only by enquiry into the bearing of revealed truths, truths to be acknowledged only by faith, on the work of the university. These are the tasks of theology, rightly understood.

So there is indeed a rationale for three of the four elements in what became in the latter part of the last century the dominant type of Catholic university curriculum: every student needs to be instructed both in some specialized discipline and also in philosophy and theology. The fourth element is a prologue to the first three. It is the acquisition or supplementation of those skills of reading and imagination, of quantitative and deductive reasoning, and of observation and experiment, and that background knowledge of the Bible, history, and nature, which, when education is in good order, are supplied by high schools. But we of course inhabit a culture in which in quite a number of ways education is not in good order. What are they? Let me consider for the moment just one.

The threat to Catholic conceptions of higher education that has always been taken seriously within Catholic universities is that which arises from rival accounts of the nature of things, rival visions of the truth about God and nature: Islamic or Buddhist visions, the materialism of the Enlightenment and its heirs, Hegelian idealism, Marburg neo-Kantianism, Marxism. Each of these in its own time and place has proposed a curriculum for universities designed to inculcate not only its own beliefs, but also a belief that the Catholic faith is a series of errors and fabrications. And the traditional apologetic stance of the Catholic thinkers was elaborated with a view to providing resources for confrontations with these rival standpoints. But this apologetic preoccupation may recently have served to distract us from a different kind of threat.

What the Catholic faith confronts today in American higher education and indeed in American education more generally is not primarily some range of alternative beliefs about the order of things, but rather a belief that there is no such thing as the order of things of which there could be a unified, if complex, understanding or even a movement toward such an understanding. There is on this contemporary view nothing to understanding except what is supplied by the specialized and professionalized disciplines and subdisciplines and subsubdisciplines. Higher education has become a set of assorted and heterogeneous specialized enquiries into a set of assorted and heterogeneous subject-matters, and general education is a set of introductions to these enquiries together with a teaching of the basic skills necessary for initiation into them, something to be got through in order to advance beyond it into the specialized disciplines. The undergraduate major, when taught by those whose training has led them to presuppose this view—for it is often taken for granted, rather than explicitly stated—becomes increasingly no more than a prologue to graduate school, even for those who will never go to graduate school. And graduate school becomes a place where narrowness of mind is inculcated as a condition for success within each particular discipline in terms defined by its senior practitioners.

All explanation is in consequence treated as if context-bound and as if there is no such thing as an integrated and integrative understanding. It is one of the ironies of contemporary academic life that some of those who are most contemptuously dismissive of postmodern theses and diagnoses behave in the practice of their own professionalized disciplines as if those theses and diagnoses were in some measure true, as if there were no context-independent standards of judgment. And the effect has been a fragmentation of the university. How far particular universities have progressed toward this fragmented condition differs from case to case. But that the major research universities of this country have steadily approximated it more and more closely is undeniable.

There is one useful touchstone by which to tell how far a particular university has moved toward this fragmented condition. Ask: Would a wonderfully effective undergraduate teacher, not only in terms of her or his own discipline, but also in terms of communicating something of how that discipline contributes to and finds its place within an integrated account of the order of things, whose scholarly contributions consisted of perhaps one original published article and some brilliant and instructive reflections on how to teach, receive tenure, promotion to full professor, and honors in that university? And would someone who is either unable or unwilling to teach any but graduate students, and preferably advanced graduate students, but who, by the standards of her or his own specialized discipline, is at what they call the cutting-edge of research enquiries, receive tenure, promotion, and honors in that university? If the answers are "No" and "Yes," then that university is in need of radical reform.

This diagnosis of the present condition of American universities enables us to identify questions that it is crucial for members of a Catholic university to ask. I begin with those that concern the place of philosophy and theology in the curriculum. What kind of discipline must philosophy be, if it is to justify retaining the place that it had in the older Catholic curriculum? It must not allow itself to be narrowed and diminished in the scope of its enquiries and it must be true to its own greatest past achievements. Characterizing the "proper nature" of philosophy—in a way that summarizes the central tradition of Catholic thinking in and about philosophy, John Paul II has spoken of the need for philosophy "to recover its *sapiential dimension* as a search for the ultimate and overarching meaning of life," so that it not only "determines the foundations and limits of the different fields of scientific learning, but will also take its place as the ultimate framework of the unity of human knowledge and action."[3] So what philosophy should be, if its own teaching and enquiries are in good order, is one and the same as it should be if it is to deserve to retain or to recover its hegemonic place in the curriculum.

The problem is that academic philosophy nowadays has itself too often degenerated into just one more specialized discipline or rather one more set of specialized subsubdisciplines, and, to the extent that this has happened, has become unable to perform its integrative tasks. Philosophy reduced to this condition gradually loses whatever place of privilege it may have had in the curriculum and in this condition deserves to lose it. But there is a mistake to be avoided here. What is wrong with philosophy is not specialization as such. Philosophy, like any discipline of substance, cannot pursue its enquiries successfully except by pursuing lines of detailed and specialized investigation. What matters is whether these do or do not contribute to philosophy's larger questions and to its always unfinished work of synthetic construction. There is therefore within any philosophical enterprise, when it is in good order, a creative tension between philosophy's unified overall concerns and its multifarious and detailed attempts to answer particular questions. Sacrifice either of these to the other and the outcome is philosophically disastrous. So the requirement that philosophy should perform its proper function within a Catholic university curriculum is not at all an external constraint imposed on academic philosophers by Catholic universities. It is simply an invitation to philosophy to be itself.

How far contemporary departments of philosophy are able to respond to this invitation adequately is a question for and about each particular department. But it is a question that has become urgent to ask. The time is overdue when each department of philosophy in a Catholic university should be compelled to justify—if it can—its right to the privilege of teaching courses prescribed for every undergraduate and to be seen to have justified that right by both faculty and students.

Theology too now stands in need of similar justification. Academic theology has also tended to become a collection of multifarious enquiries, and academic distinction within each of these has little or nothing to do with ability to perform those integrative tasks that are central to theology's function within and on behalf of a Catholic university. What theology has to respond to in the first instance are the incompleteness and the limitations of a purely philosophical view of the order of things: it has to show us nature from the standpoint of grace. And theologians will be unable to achieve this, unless they too are and have been trained as philosophers. We badly need now to move toward a condition often taken for granted in the past, in which philosophy is integral to every theological education. Conversely, philosophers will be unable to perform their tasks in a Catholic university adequately until they are able to view themselves and their discipline in the light afforded by a theology of revelation. And these changes are of the first importance not only for those engaged in enquiry at the contemporary cutting edge, but also and as much for those instructing students in the elements of the Catholic faith, in the catechism. Students, understandably, are apt to view instruction into the truths of the Catholic faith as just one more kind of instruction, to be set alongside other secular kinds, instruction that has its own peculiar importance, but that could be subtracted from the curriculum without any loss to those other secular kinds. And insofar as they encounter theology only as a set of specialized disciplines, this immature view will be reinforced. What those students have to learn is that, from the standpoint of a Catholic university, education in physics or history or economics remains incomplete until it is to some degree illuminated by philosophical enquiry, and all education, including their philosophical education, is incomplete until it is illuminated by theologically grounded insight.

I take it, therefore, that both philosophy and theology, when in good order, should find a required place in the studies with which both undergraduate and graduate education culminate rather than being restricted, as they now so often are, to introductory classes. That both disciplines also have an important introductory role is certainly true. But their restriction to such a role would make it impossible for them to discharge their proper function. And this has implications for both undergraduate and graduate education.

Secular universities today structure their curricula so that the movement is almost uniformly from the broad and general to the narrow and specialized. Undergraduate students move from general introductory courses in a number of disciplines toward the specializations of the major, while graduate students move from already specialized courses in a number of subdisciplines toward the narrowly focused research of their dissertations, perhaps an adequate preparation for a career to be spent exclusively in the same kind of research, but a remarkably inadequate education for anything else, including the life of a university teacher. It is not in question, of course, that we teachers have to be trained as specialized researchers and that some of us—not necessarily all of us—have to continue to engage in such research. The point is that we have to learn to understand what we do as specialized researchers in context, and education into that context is almost never supplied. To supply it we would have to reform all our Ph.D. programs by adding to them both a theological and a philosophical dimension, so that the training of future college and university teachers is informed by the same integrative perspective that is required in undergraduate education.

2. Two Alternative Directions for Catholic Universities

Catholic universities thus face an interesting choice: *either* they should require *more* philosophy and theology courses than they do now *or* they should abolish their requirements for such courses altogether. To choose the latter alternative would be to reject the dominant older conception of what a Catholic university is and should be in favor of a very different conception, a conception of a Catholic university as a place where the activities of a secular university and Catholic religious practice happen to coexist within a single institution, one in which a significant proportion of the practitioners of the specialized disciplines happen also to be Catholics. The responsibilities of the faculty in such a university would consist only of their teaching, their research, and their advising and administrative duties. The standards by which they would be evaluated would be solely those of each particular academic profession, and specialized research would have the same place that it has in the great secular research universities. There would be no official faculty responsibility of any kind for performing those integrative tasks that were traditionally assigned to philosophers and theologians. And so there would be no privileged place accorded to the teaching of philosophy and theology. In such universities the question would often arise for particular individual faculty members of how their faith relates to their academic studies and teaching, and enterprises designed to pursue this question would recurrently flourish. But such enterprises would necessarily be marginal to the projects that would be in practice treated as central to the life of such universities, although this might be masked from the outside world by that rhetoric which is the required stock-in-trade of university officials.

Here, then, are two rival conceptions of a Catholic university, one in which the university recognizes itself as Catholic, not only because of its religious practices, but because of the philosophical and theological dimensions of its teaching and its enquiries, and the other in which a Catholic university is a standard secular university to which Catholic religious practices together with a set of individual Catholic academic concerns have been superadded. Two further differences between these rival conceptions are worth noting.

The first concerns the way in which each answers the question: To whom should a Catholic university be accountable and for what? For this second conception, accountability in purely academic matters would be one thing, accountability for religious and pastoral practice quite another. Accountability to the church, and more particularly to the local bishop, for the latter would be uncontroversial. Accountability to the church for the former would make little sense. And it would not matter whether there was or was not a preponderance of Catholic faculty. But on the first and more traditional conception of a Catholic university, accountability to the church in respect of both the teaching of philosophy and more especially the teaching of theology would be a condition of a Catholic university's integrity. And it would be crucial that there should be a preponderance of Catholic faculty members just because it is in the end only the faculty who can secure the Catholic identity of a university and determine what kind of identity it is and what its forms of academic expression should be. The primary expressions of any university's identity are in its classrooms and laboratories. In a Catholic university what matters most is the relationship between what is said and done in the classroom or laboratory and what happens at Mass and in the life of prayer. And that relationship depends upon the Catholic faculty. It is also of course of crucial importance that there should be non-Catholic faculty in Catholic universities, not only because of the excellence of what such faculty can contribute, but also in order to prevent Catholics from forgetting that the secular calling of the university *qua* university is shared with non-Catholics and that non-Catholic scholars may and often do respect that calling with more integrity than some Catholics do.

It is then primarily the Catholic faculty and only secondarily officials and administrators who need to be held accountable to and by the teaching church and this not only, but especially in respect of the teaching of philosophy and theology. A Catholic university's accountability to the church in respect of philosophy should be that of showing not only that the university has made provision for the performance of philosophy's integrative tasks, but that it has done so in accordance with the prescriptions of and in the spirit of the encyclical *Faith and Reason.* In respect of theology the university should be similarly accountable, but also for showing that the theology informing its teaching accords with the teaching of episcopal and papal authority. And such accountability should not be understood as a matter of externally imposed constraints, but rather as a happy recognition by the university of its Catholicity. Such accountability could of course take a number of different forms, and to argue in favor of it is not to argue in favor of any one such form. A welcome first step in giving institutional form to this accountability was taken by the Catholic bishops of the United States in their statement of November 1999, in response to *Ex corde ecclesiae.* But it needs to be emphasized that this was only a first step and that how the provisions of that statement are implemented will depend upon continuing and extended dialogue between the bishops and the Catholic colleges and universities, by which I do not mean merely dialogue between the bishops and college and university officials and administrators. And, if this dialogue is sustained, it will itself play a key part in determining which of the two conceptions of a Catholic university that I have been outlining prevails in the Catholic academic community.

Consider yet another respect in which the two different conceptions of a Catholic university that I have been contrasting are at odds, namely, the kind of attention to the writings of St. Thomas Aquinas that is taken to be appropriate. For those who hold the more recent view, Aquinas will have become just one more figure in the history of thought, even if an unusually distinguished one. But for those who hold to the older view it will be important to recall, both when thinking about the curriculum and elsewhere, the declaration of John Paul II, reiterating assertions of many earlier popes, that "the Church has been justified in consistently proposing Saint Thomas as a master of thought."[4] At a variety of key points in theology, philosophy, and elsewhere, systematic dialogue with Aquinas will be on this view a distinctive mark of Catholic enquiry and teaching. And, since such dialogue requires the presence of Thomists, Thomists will be needed in such a university, although other theological and philosophical voices, Catholic and non-Catholic, will also need to be heard.

Note that what I have been comparing so far are two conceptions best envisaged as ideal types, types defining extreme points of a spectrum along which particular modern Catholic universities at particular periods in their history can be ranged. What is important to emphasize is that the movement of particular universities in one direction or the other along this spectrum will have different types of causes, depending upon the direction in which a particular university is moving. Movements toward that end of the spectrum at which Catholic universities order their curriculum and their enquiries toward the integrative tasks of philosophy and theology will never take place without deliberate planning by both faculty and administrators. But movement toward the other end of the spectrum may on occasion be planned, but in the absence of planning will occur anyway, as a result of the natural drift of contemporary academic culture, unless drastic countermeasures are taken. Appoint to a Catholic university a sufficiently large proportion of faculty members who are committed to the kind of career success that would make them eligible for distinguished appointments in prestigious secular research universities and, almost inevitably, what you will produce is a Catholic university that is in central respects no more than a replica, although always a significantly inferior replica, of those secular universities.

It is also worth remarking that Catholic scholars will generally have no good reason for preferring working in a Catholic university of this latter kind to working in a secular academic environment, perhaps in one of those research universities which this type of Catholic university is so assiduously trying to emulate. It will of course be important to such scholars that there should be a lively Catholic community within their university and that there should be sufficient opportunities to show their students what it is to have a Catholic intellectual vocation. But there are secular universities in which both these conditions can be satisfied. And so a crucial question is posed: Insofar as Catholic universities move or have moved toward that end of the spectrum in which they have assimilated themselves, so far as possible, to the great secular research universities, what point is there in any continuing claim to distinctiveness as Catholic universities? The answer is surely, little or none.

3. Education for Making Choices

The argument so far has suggested that one principal danger to Catholic universities arises from their faculty. A second large danger arises from their students. Catholic universities in America have always been places of upward mobility and happily so. It is undeniably important that students should recognize that there is work waiting for them to do and that they are preparing themselves to inhabit the world of work. But a university education, according to *any* adequate conception, is not, except incidentally, a training in the skills that are needed in various kinds of work. And here I am speaking about the teaching of all those specialized disciplines that deserve a place in an undergraduate curriculum. What a university education plays its distinctive part by providing is the kind of understanding that has to be valued for its own sake and not for those incidental benefits. That understanding is to be achieved through study of those disciplines that comprise the liberal arts, including the natural sciences. Nothing else should find a place in undergraduate teaching.

It is essential to the flourishing of the liberal arts and sciences that their teachers should be devoted to them as a set of complementary disciplines and not just to their own particular discipline. For the value of each particular discipline lies in key part in its contribution to the overall enterprise of a liberal education, and this needs to be recognized. One minimal way in which such recognition can be achieved is exemplified in those universities in which, on faculty curriculum committees and on faculty tenure and promotion committees, historians and philosophers have to explain the significance of their research and justify the approval of their courses to neurobiologists, physicists, and economists, and vice versa. For without such interchanges you endanger the possibility of recognizing the significance of the liberal arts and sciences as such, a significance bound up with their character as the arts and sciences of a free human being. What then makes the liberal arts and sciences liberal?

What the liberal arts and sciences are designed to achieve for students is the liberation of their minds from preconceptions imposed upon them by the established culture. This liberation is achieved in stages. There is first of all an acquisition of skills that requires focused attention, and a care for, as Newman said, clearness, accuracy, and precision, the first form that a love of truth takes, so that students are able to respond to the questions: What do you mean? From what premises does your conclusion follow? What rule did you follow? What did you observe? In a culture in which education was in good order, this stage of a liberal education would have occurred in high school.[5] But in North America today part of this work of the high school often has to be done in colleges and universities. For those who are still unable to answer these elementary questions are not yet qualified to proceed further in a progress designed to achieve a transformation of students, so that they learn to see, to imagine, to understand, and to speak from a variety of hitherto alien standpoints: to see what Turner saw and Cassatt saw, to imagine what Sophocles and Shakespeare and Dickinson imagined, to understand as Aristotle and Newton and Bohr understood and also as Thucydides and Gibbon understood. In a Catholic university a central task at this second stage is to introduce the student to a variety of culturally diverse forms of specifically Catholic achievement: to Giotto and Bernini, to Dante and Racine, to Hopkins and Shusako Endo and Flannery O'Connor, to Augustine and Aquinas and Newman and Edith Stein. And such an education, if it is successful, will enable its students to view themselves and the world in a new and unexpected light. They will have a different and enlarged understanding of the multiplicity of human goods and of *the* human good.

So the liberal arts and sciences not only introduce us to new experiences and activities, teaching us to value them for their own sake; they also prepare us for making intelligent choices. Until students have understood what the various liberal arts and sciences have to teach, they lack resources for recognizing in many types of situations what the alternatives are between which they have to choose, what goods are at stake in the choice of one alternative rather than another, what it is about themselves that is relevant to the making of good or bad choices, and what the significance of their choices is in the order of things. And without such recognitions our liberty of choice will be in part an illusion. We will be the victims of influences upon us that we have not adequately understood.

It is therefore always a serious mistake for students to approach the study of the liberal arts, thinking that they already know what their studies should lead to, to what ends they should be a means. For to think that is to suppose that they could prior to those studies have made adequately informed and intelligent decisions about what for them constitutes a choiceworthy way of life. But just this mistake is now made by that very large number of American students who approach higher education believing that its overriding purpose is to get them some already identified kind of job, the achievement of which will be a mark of worldly success. They have made some of their key choices prematurely. And increasingly universities have made a corresponding mistake. They have responded all too positively to an invitation to treat students as consumers to whose demand they ought to be responsive. But it is a primary responsibility of a university to be unresponsive, to give its students what they need, not what they want, and to do so in such a way that what they want becomes what they need and what they choose is choice-worthy.

Here again Catholic universities confront alternatives: either to hold fast to an older conception of higher education or instead to surrender to powerful contemporary trends. And once again it will require positive efforts to sustain and strengthen the choice in a university that is faithful to that older conception, while inaction will almost inevitably lead to a surrender of the university to market forces. But here what is at stake is nothing less than the character of our present and future alumni. Do we really want them to become what, on the best evidence that we have, recent graduates of the best research universities have tended to become: narrowly focused professionals, immensely and even obsessionally hard working, disturbingly competitive and intent on success as it is measured within their own specialized professional sphere, often genuinely excellent at what they do; who read little worthwhile that is not relevant to their work; who, as the idiom insightfully puts it, "make time," sometimes with difficulty, for their family lives; and whose relaxation tends to consist of short strenuous bouts of competitive athletic activity and sometimes of therapeutic indulgence in the kind of religion that is well designed not to disrupt their working lives?[6]

One danger for such alumni, whether Catholic or otherwise, is that they fall victim to an increasingly salient feature of our society, perhaps of all societies in the condition of advanced modernity. I call this feature compartmentalization. A compartmentalized society has two distinctive characteristics. Each of the separate spheres of activity through which individuals pass in the course of a day or a week or a month has its own distinctive culture, its own modes of relationship, its own specific norms. And in each of these spheres individuals can function effectively only by presenting themselves in and through whatever roles they occupy in this or that particular sphere. So as individuals pass from home and family to workplace to school to leisure-time activities and to political or religious associations, they become adroit in leaving behind the roles, norms, and attitudes appropriate to the sphere that they have just left and assuming those of the sphere that they are about to enter. They present themselves through their roles as one kind of person in the home, another in the workplace, a third in the social club. And so in extreme cases the individual is nearly, if not quite, dissolved into the set of roles that she or he plays.

A second distinctive characteristic of social compartmentalization reinforces these same effects. There is increasingly nowhere within compartmentalized societies in which individuals are invited in a practically effective way to view their lives as a whole, to evaluate themselves and those qualities that belong to them as individuals, the virtues and the vices, rather than those that belong to them as successful or unsuccessful role-players. In the past a variety of institutions, both religious and secular, have provided milieus within which individuals and groups were able to stand back from their everyday lives and judge themselves critically by a standard of human goodness external to and independent of those of the various spheres of activity in which they were engaged. And it was one of the works of the Catholic faith, and more especially of Catholic education, to provide within just such milieus an integrative vision of the human and natural orders, as well as of the supernatural order, one that could inform not only education, but the subsequent lives of the educated, by providing them with a standard for identifying and criticizing the inadequacies of the social orders that they inhabited. Why is it of the first importance that Catholic schools, colleges, and universities should still provide such milieus?

It is not only because we need to provide our students with an alternative to the narrowly restrictive understanding of the values of social life that compartmentalization imposes. It is also because of the values that dominate so much of the life of the secular world that those students are preparing to enter, values that have already influenced them before they enter upon their college education. Howard R. Greene has listed what his survey of four thousand undergraduates showed to be the goals shared by students in public and private colleges: "making a good deal of money, being in a position of personal power, marrying the right person, having good friends, using the educational advantages that they received."[7] And Greene provides elsewhere in his book abundant evidence of the extent to which an undergraduate education is viewed as primarily and perhaps even sometimes no more than a means to further professional training that will provide the basis for achieving these goals. As Robert H. Frank and Philip J. Cook have written, "If access to the top jobs depends more and more on educational credentials, we would expect [students] to do everything in their power to improve their credentials and indeed they have."[8]

And this is perhaps not surprising. For the cost of higher education is now such that both students and their parents have learned to view their expenditure as an investment, and the choice of college or university, the attempt to maximize one's GPA, and the choice of major and of graduate or professional schools are all to a remarkable extent directed by a wish to see as high a return on that investment as possible.

Consider just one effect. Greene has reported that "my many conversations with undergraduates and recent graduates have confirmed the influence that their finances play in choosing careers. Once they have tallied the debts that they will have to repay, a number of talented young adults are abandoning earlier plans to enter education, the public sector, social science, and other low-paying careers."[9] Such students, we may note, have given their allegiance to those educationalists about whom Newman wrote that "they insist that Education should be confined to some particular and narrow end, and should issue in some definite work, which can be weighed and measured. They argue as if every thing, as well as every person, had its price; and that where there has been a great outlay, they have a right to expect a return in kind."[10] The return that so many of our contemporaries have learned to expect is of course not only financial, even if in the United States money remains the most widely recognized and the most generally corrupting form of success. Success is also conceived of in terms of power, prestige, and celebrity, and it is often alumni who have achieved success in just these terms who are honored by their colleges and universities and wooed with an eye to some munificent contribution to the endowment. So the view among undergraduates that their education is no more than a means to an end that can be adequately conceived prior to and independently of that education is dangerously reinforced.

Since it is one of the tasks of the teaching of the liberal arts and sciences to correct this misunderstanding, such teaching, if effective, will be bound to put in question the currently dominant notion of what constitutes success. But in order to be effective in so doing, it will have to avoid or circumvent the effects of compartmentalization within universities, including Catholic universities. For only students whose education has enabled them to integrate the different aspects of what they have learned, so that each can be put, whenever relevant, to the tasks of understanding, including the tasks of understanding their own place in the order of things, will be qualified to make the choices that will confront them throughout their subsequent lives. But note that what has to be so integrated is what has been learned in all the different areas of the university's life: in the language laboratory and in the chapel, on the basketball court and in the library, in the social relationships of the residence hall and in those of the philosophy seminar. And therefore among the obstacles to integrated learning and to adequate choice-making that students have to overcome is any rigid compartmentalization of their lives into what are so often now treated as autonomous areas, both in the society at large and in universities, even in Catholic universities.

Compartmentalization is sometimes so pervasive a phenomenon that we may not notice its negative effects. Those effects, I have suggested, include an uncritical attitude toward the norms and values of each particular compartmentalized area, arising from an inability to bring to bear what has been learned in each such area of one's life upon the activities of other areas. So the classroom may be treated as a place for a rigorous testing of ideas, while conversation outside the classroom remains mindless and philistine. So the chapel may be treated as the place where the significance of one's life is disclosed, while this disclosure is for the most part ignored in other areas of the university's life. So the modes of athletic activity may proceed without regard to anything that happens in classroom or chapel. And to the extent that student social life is thus compartmentalized, no reform of the curriculum that aims to provide an integrative education is likely to be successful.

It is of crucial importance, for example, that learning should go on not only in class, but between classes; that when students come into the classroom, they should bring with them questions and reflections that they have developed since the last class; and that those questions and reflections should have been developed through informal discussion with their fellow students, most often with those taking the same courses, but sometimes with those not taking the same courses. That is to say, it is important that what goes on in the classroom provides a leaven for student conversation in every area. And what holds for students holds, although in a somewhat different way, for faculty. It is of crucial importance for integrative education that faculty members who are teachers of literature or history should understand what is at stake in making or having failed to make the truths of evolutionary biology or the equations of quantum mechanics part of one's view of the world, and that physicists and biologists should care about Shakespeare and Mozart, so that there is a continuing conversation between the practitioners of different disciplines.

(Experience teaches us that for narrowness in this respect it is not usually the natural scientists, but the self-styled humanists whom we have to fear.) For otherwise how can faculty members genuinely care about the curriculum as a whole rather than merely about their own discipline or subdiscipline?

Here we need to remind ourselves of the effect that certain types of enquiry can have in promoting this kind of conversation between both faculty and students. Consider that remarkable book by the Trinidadian Marxist of genius, C. L. R. James, *Beyond a Boundary*.[11] James's book is at once a history and a celebration of cricket and of its place in the life of the West Indies and also a history and a celebration of that moral tradition in England, the West Indies, and elsewhere which has informed the history of cricket. So it is a book about Thomas Arnold of Rugby School as well as about such great cricketers as W. G. Grace and Frank Worrell. American students, seldom knowing anything about cricket, would of course find it initially difficult to learn what James has to teach. For James had himself been a cricketer and it matters that he was able to write about cricket not only as a historian, but out of his lifelong practical engagement with cricket. But what James's book can do even for Americans—and I know no other book of the same quality—is to provide a model for how to think about games and their place in human life together with those who actually have the athletic skills and play the games.

It is a disgrace to any university to have football or basketball or baseball players or coaches who are not deeply engaged academically, and genuine academic engagement, for anyone who takes these games seriously, involves thinking about these games in moral, social, and historical contexts. So we have in James's history one example of the kind of integrative education that might enable us to overcome, even if in small ways, some of the threats presented by compartmentalization. James of course was only able to achieve what he did because of his Marxist perspective. The challenge to us is to make sure from our Catholic perspective that we can see at least as much as he saw from his Marxist point of view by integrating Marxist truths and insights into our account of the order of things.

We have then identified still further questions to raise about the curriculum. For we not only need what theology and philosophy can provide and what the liberal arts and sciences can supply, but must meet those needs in a way that will enable our students to rethink themselves and their aims and choices. Catholic education has to supply not the means to conventionally conceived success, but a set of experiences through which students become able to put that conception of success in question and to direct themselves toward other goals.

4. Whose Choices?

I have tried to present in this paper two alternative directions in which contemporary American Catholic universities can move: *either* toward a retrieval of a kind of Catholic identity that will not only inform every aspect of the university's life, but will enable it to function as a genuine university, *or* toward increasing assimilation to the conditions of the currently most prestigious American research universities and a consequent replication of their fragmented condition. And I have suggested that, while deliberate planning and decision making will be necessary for movement in the former direction, inertia and inaction will be sufficient to continue movement in the latter direction, a direction that is inimical to everything that gives a Catholic university or college its distinctive value. It will not of course generally be any one large decision that will determine which of these two roads is taken, but rather a series of smaller decisions on particular matters. And how those decisions are made and by whom will make a significant difference to the character of the changes that they bring about. For the decisions that matter most will be those made by the faculty and the changes that matter most will be those in which the faculty are primarily involved.

Presidents, provosts, and deans will therefore have to learn how to speak for and not only to their faculties and to recognize that the decisions now confronting Catholic universities cannot be imposed upon either a recalcitrant or a passive faculty without having quite other than their intended effects. Indeed the very habit of mind that lends university administrators—and in consequence faculty too—to think of "the administration" as one thing and "the faculty" as another is a harmful obstacle to the kind of conversation now necessary. Only presidents, provosts, and deans who are actively members of the faculty (still regularly reading and teaching and thinking, as faculty members do, even if only for a small part of their working week), who think of themselves as such, and who are thought of by their faculty as such, will be able to act constructively in this situation. It is therefore not only the faculty and the students of Catholic universities who are on occasion a threat. Administrators too are apt to endanger the institutions that they aspire to serve.

The possibility that wrong choices will be made is very real. But to have become aware that this is a time of inescapable choice and of the consequences of choosing wrongly is itself to have made a first step toward choosing rightly. This is a time of danger, but it is also a time of hope.

NOTES

1. John Henry Newman, *The Idea of a University*, VI, 6.
2. *Ex corde ecclesiae*, 15, 16.
3. *Faith and Reason*, 81.
4. Ibid, 43.
5. Newman, *The Idea of a University*, II, iv, 1.
6. See, for example, Herant Katchadourian and John Boli, *The Cream of the Crop: The Impact of Elite Education in the Decade after College* (New York: Basic Books, 1994).
7. Howard R. Greene, *The Select: Realities of Life and Learning in America's Elite Colleges* (New York: Cliff Street Books, 1998), 202.
8. Robert H. Frank and Philip J. Cook, *The Winner-Take-All Society: Why the Few at the Top Get So Much More Than the Rest of Us* (New York: Free Press, 1995), as quoted in ibid, xxi.
9. Greene, *The Select*, 72.
10. Newman, *The Idea of a University*, VII, 2.
11. C.L.R. James, *Beyond a Boundary* (London: Hutchinson, 1983).

2

Catholicism and Sociology

Elective Affinity
or Unholy Alliance?

ALAN WOLFE

1. The Reality of Coexistence

Were Catholicism and sociology ever meant to coexist, peacefully or otherwise? The question is worth asking because both have experienced somewhat similar fates in recent years. Sociology and Catholicism have each had Golden Ages in the past but have also run into hard times: it is as difficult to get first-class students to major in sociology at most American universities as it is for most Catholic elementary and secondary schools to recruit their teachers from within the church. Yet both sociology and Catholicism—however numerous the detractors who take a certain pleasure in their problems—have survived, often at the margins of what is considered respectable, yet with sufficient adherents so that neither can be ignored. This in turn gives members of each a similar outlook on the world: occasionally embattled and defensive, but nonetheless convinced that their enterprise contains a truth to which the world had best pay attention.

To juxtapose sociology and Catholicism might nonetheless strike strong adherents of each as somewhat bizarre. Over the two thousand years in which Catholicism has existed, only the last hundred have been coterminous with sociology, which suggests that the church has gotten along fine for 95 percent of its history without any reliance whatsoever on what sociology has to offer. The juxtaposition also sounds odd from the sociological side for at least two reasons. One is that sociology often understands itself, especially in its Durkheimian form, as something of a secular religion. For Durkheim the majesty of religion was testimony, not to God's power, but to the human imagination. And secondly, to the degree that sociology became intertwined with religion nonetheless, as it no doubt did even in its Durkheimian dimensions, Catholicism was not its religion of choice. The other great founder of the discipline, Max Weber, not only was Protestant, but was especially attracted to the ideas of that former priest, Martin Luther, who, from a Catholic viewpoint, began all that trouble. Weber took from Luther one of his most important concepts, that of a vocation. And, of course, he never wrote a book on the "Catholic Ethic and the Spirit of Capitalism." To the degree that Weber was influenced by Catholicism it was a negative influence: as John McGreevy, citing the historian David Blackbourn, reminds us, *The Protestant Ethic and the Spirit of Capitalism* was a by-product of Germany's Kulturkampf, a late addition to the idea that Catholicism was a force for backwardness.[1]

Whatever the elective affinity between Protestantism and sociology in Germany, moreover, it seemed easily transportable to the United States. Nearly all of the great founders of American sociology—Charles Horton Cooley, George Herbert Mead, Albion Small—were Protestant. Indeed, most of them grew up with fathers who were ministers in various Protestant denominations. Arthur Vidich and Sanford Lyman view the development of American sociology as a form of displaced Protestantism,[2] a view that perhaps helps to explain Talcott Parsons's concern with an alleged "authoritarian element in the basic structure of the Catholic church itself which may weaken individual self-reliance and valuation of freedom."[3]

The tensions between sociology and Catholicism can be multiplied. The church understood itself as universal in its aspirations. But sociology could not exist without the concept of culture, which is, by definition, particularistic. Given a large group of people, the sociologist wants immediately to categorize them into those features of ethnicity, race, language, and history that make them distinct. Given the same group of people, the Catholic wants to find out whether they can all find a way to believe in the same God, and in roughly the same way. To be sure, the church eventually dropped Latin in favor of the vernacular, but that was long after sociology— itself reflective of an increasing sense of national pride—had come into existence. Sociologists tend to reify borders. Catholics tend to cross them.

And if these were not differences enough, the sociologist and the Catholic adhere to very different conceptions of truth. Of course in a postmodern age when a large number of theorists question whether anything can be said to be true, the fact that both the social sciences and a number of religious traditions claim the possibility of truth-telling gives them something in common. But we cannot forget how different their conceptions of truth are. The sociologist seeks an empirical truth, one that generally establishes itself through some form of experimentation borrowed from the natural sciences; truth, in that sense, is contained in a proper interpretation of relevant data. Many leading Catholic thinkers, by contrast, reflect Leo XIII's insistence on natural law premises as the basis for Catholic theology. Underlying these different conceptions of truth are different views on human nature. Natural law conceptions of truth, more timeless and transcendental than the provisional truths established with the help of correlation coefficients, appeal to the consistency of human nature, while sociologists are given to proclaiming its plasticity. One does not have to read very far into a text dealing with any contemporary issue before one knows whether numbers are meant to decide an issue or whether deductions are formulated in the mode of Thomas Acquinas. To cite John McGreevy again: "Whereas Ernest W. Burgess and Robert E. Park defined sociology as an 'experimental science,' one Catholic sociologist"—his name is Paul Hanley Furfey—"defiantly called for a 'supernatural sociology' since divine revelation can contribute certain pertinent social data which are enormously important and which could be learned in no other way."[4]

With all these differences, one might be tempted to conclude that there is not, nor need there ever be, a relationship between sociology and Catholicism. If so, I could bring my discussion to an end at this point. However, I am saved by the organizers of this volume. For they called it "Higher Learning and Catholic Traditions," and it is worthwhile noting that of these two topics which bring us together, only the latter is cast in the plural. This suggests that there is no one Catholic tradition against which sociology can be contrasted. So let me add from the sociological side—assuming, which some would contest, that my discipline is part of the higher learning—that there is also no one sociological tradition against which Catholicism can be contrasted. Instead of a dialogue of the deaf between Catholicism and sociology, we are much more likely to witness intersections between some Catholic traditions and some sociological traditions. And, that is exactly what we have witnessed in recent decades in this country.

One reason why sociology and Catholicism have managed to coexist is that they do so in a particularly American environment. Among the many

Catholic traditions is an American one.[5] Once Catholicism learned that it could expose itself to America and still be Catholic, it learned that it could also expose itself to sociology and still be Catholic. Both changed themselves in the process, which is another way of saying that both Americanized themselves in the process. Sociology, when it came to America, dropped the Sturm und Drang romantic pessimism of European social thought in favor of what Robert Merton would come to call middle-range theory. Catholicism, when it came to America, would transform many anti-modernist aspects of the church and its teachings into an eminently practical effort to build institutions that would respond, not only to the spiritual needs of modern-day Catholics, but to their everyday needs as well. Symbolizing the mutual effect that each had on the other is the fact that one of the classic works of sociology, *The Polish Peasant in Europe and America*, took as its theme the transformation occurring among Catholics as they came to this country and in the process helped transform sociology into an empirical discipline.[6] Both sociology and Catholicism, in a sense, met American pragmatism and survived by incorporating a good deal of its spirit. As difficult as it may be to imagine sociology and Catholicism flourishing together in, say, Belgium—or even in the Poland from which all those peasants came—there was no problem finding common ground in the United States.

Sociology and Catholicism also became intertwined in the United States because both found themselves preoccupied with the social question. This was also true in Europe. The same social disruptions that led sociologists to talk about gemeinschaft and gesellschaft led Catholics to talk about *Rerum Novarum* and *Quadragesimo Anno*. But in America a similar focus on social questions was linked to the fact that both sociology and Catholicism were urban phenomena; indeed, both flourished in the same quintessentially urban city called Chicago. The development of academic sociology cannot be separated from its relationship with social work, symbolized by the close cooperation between the "Chicago School" of Robert Ezra Park and the Hull House of Jane Addams. In a similar way, the National Catholic Welfare Conference of Msgr. John A. Ryan—the "Right Reverend New Dealer," as he was known by his critics—was an essential component of the growth of the church in the 1920s and 1930s. Sociology's typical left-wing bias, at least on economic questions, is not an obstacle to cooperation with Catholicism.

No wonder, given the mutually overlapping concerns of Catholicism and sociology, that nearly all Catholic colleges and universities have departments of sociology. The one that exists at the University of Notre Dame is especially highly regarded, and nothing in the Catholic character of Notre Dame has prevented it from seeking empirical truths using the latest methodologies that one would find at any secular university. Geography is, in any case, a more powerful determinant of academic culture in America than religion: What differentiates sociology departments is not whether they are public and secular or private and faith-based, but whether, for example, they are in the East or the Midwest. Hence Notre Dame's sociology department has more in common with the sociologists at the University of Michigan than it does with the sociologists at my own institution, Boston College—and Boston College's department, in turn, resembles that of Brandeis more than it does that of Chapel Hill.

Sociology contains as many traditions as Catholicism, and some have been more appealing to Catholic traditions than others. Durkheim may have been Jewish, but many leading Durkheimians were Catholic: E. E. Evans-Pritchard, Mary Douglas, and Victor Turner did not develop their interest in ritual and symbol in a vacuum.[7] At one point, Catholic sociologists in America had their own specifically Catholic professional association and their own journal, and even when both became more ecumenical, there remained enough of a tradition of "Catholic sociology" to include Andrew Greeley and William V. D'Antonio. In *After Virtue*, Alasdair MacIntyre writes that "a moral philosophy presupposes a sociology" and that the sociologist par excellence of our emotivist time is Erving Goffman, a statement with which I find myself in full agreement.[8] By its very nature, the quantitative tradition in sociology has no special affinity with any religious tradition; it can be used—or shunned—by all of them. But that is not true of many of the theoretical traditions in sociology. Charles Taylor's work in particular can be read as an effort by a philosopher to rewrite the history of sociology in order to highlight the degree to which human action is shaped by forces outside the rational control of any one actor—and in that way to suggest that humanistic traditions in sociology have more to tell us than traditions borrowed from biology or economics.[9]

When it comes to the relationship between sociology and Catholicism, in short, we face one of those discrepancies between theory and practice on which sociology feeds. In theory, a religious tradition as venerable, hierarchical, deductive, normative, and secure in its faith as Catholicism ought to have little or nothing in common with an academic tradition as modern, egalitarian, analytic, objective, and technical as contemporary sociology. Yet because they do live together, the most important question to ask about them is how they might make the conditions of their coexistence more beneficial to each other. For they do not always get along in ways that encourage the strengths of what each tradition has to offer. Let me try to illustrate this by means of an example of great interest both to sociology and to Catholicism: the question of whether in recent years the United States has experienced a decline in its moral bearings serious enough to raise profound and disturbing questions about the way we live now.

2. America's Moral Decline

It has become a staple of both contemporary social science and social criticism that America faces a serious moral deficit. One well-known proponent of this point of view is former Secretary of Education William Bennett. From a wide variety of sources—the Bible, great literature, children's stories, history—Western societies, he believes, came to a broad agreement on the importance of the virtues. But if such virtues as friendship, loyalty, work, and faith are not taught well, especially to the young, they turn into vices. Bennett leaves no doubt that such vices are omnipresent in contemporary America. Surveying the moral landscape, he is disturbed by rising rates of divorce, out-of-wedlock births, crime, and other potential indicators of decline. Indeed, once one starts looking for them, signs of moral degeneration seem to be everywhere: basketball players strangling their coaches; cadets at austere military institutions participating in cheating rings; the entertainment industry purveying sex and violence to ever younger watchers and listeners; gays demanding acceptance of their sexuality; and, most disturbing of all, a president engaging in sordid and illicit sex and then lying about it on television and in the courts. Moral health is like physical health: to find out whether the body is sick, you take its temperature. And no matter how you measure it, Bennett believes, America's moral illness gets worse day by day. A society in which vice triumphs over virtue is morally flabby: we do what is in our best interest, shirk our responsibilities when they prove burdensome, lie to get ahead, and, as afraid of administering punishment as having it administered, persuade ourselves that everyone deserves a second—or third or fourth—chance.[10]

The fact that William Bennett is Catholic in no way makes his analysis Catholic; one can find similar complaints about America's moral health from Protestant and Jewish writers. But Bennett, who has made Hollywood a particular focus of his concerns, does carry forward a specific American Catholic concern with morality like that embodied in the Hays Office—not to mention that his views overlap with the pronouncements of Francis Cardinal Spellman and the writings of William F. Buckley Jr. No American religious denomination has a monopoly on morality, but students of American society have generally taken second- and third-generation Catholics as a model for adherence to more culturally conservative moral norms. A recent example is offered by the journalist Alan Ehrenhalt.[11] He invokes the moral world of Chicago in the 1940s and 1950s—populated in large part by the children of those Polish peasants who arrived in America only to undergo the scrutiny of sociologists—as embodying a respect for moral authority missing in America today. Catholics kept alive more than Jewish or Protestant immigrants the gemeinschaft character of their villages even while living in American cities, which is why Herbert Gans identified them as "urban villagers."[12]

We know, thanks to the work of sociologists Robert Wuthnow and James Davison Hunter, that specific religious denominations count for less in America than attitudes toward modernity: conservative Catholics have more in common politically with conservative Protestants than they do with liberal Catholics.[13] When voices are raised in American public debate, moreover, they are more likely to be dismissed as sectarian if identified with a specific faith. For all these reasons, we are unlikely to find a distinctly "Catholic" outlook on America's current moral crisis. Yet because of Catholicism's particular history in the United States, it should not surprise us that many of the most articulate defenders of the idea that America has lost its moral bearing speak in recognizably Catholic tones: James Q. Wilson, Richard John Neuhaus, George Weigel, John DiIulio Jr., Robert George, the Genoveses, and, in this volume, Mary Ann Glendon and, in her distinctly almost-Catholic manner, Jean Bethke Elshtain. Each of these individuals has written about morality in America in different ways, so it would not be correct to say that they all embody one particular tradition, let alone a particularly Catholic one. But it seems undeniable to me that one of the most important Catholic traditions in America—the one that insists on fairly strict adherence to time-tested moral precepts—has been part and parcel of America's recent concern with its moral health.

The same holds for sociology. Just as thinkers motivated by religious concerns have entered the debate over morality in America, so have social

scientists motivated by questions raised by classic thinkers in the sociological tradition such as de Tocqueville and Durkheim. None has gotten
as much attention as the political scientist Robert Putnam.[14] Had Putnam
found, as many political scientists have, that Americans no longer vote to
the extent they once did or have dropped their identification with political parties, there would have been little concern with his research, because
we have traditionally been suspicious of formal politics. But Tocqueville
wrote that we took pride in matters closer to home, such as voluntary associations and communities. If there was a fall-off in interest and activity
there, then what is put into question is the whole idea that America is a
society specially blessed by the "self-interest rightly understood" of its
citizens.

And that is precisely what Putnam apparently discovered. Organizations which had once seemed to symbolize the vibrancy of American civic
and associational life—Kiwanis clubs, parent and teacher associations,
and, of course, the by now famous bowling leagues—all were experiencing significant declines in membership. And those were not the only ones.
Labor unions, which had once been viewed by sociologists as instrumental
in teaching democratic values, were in decline. The General Social Survey, Putnam pointed out, reported sharp fall-offs in church attendance.
Volunteers for the Boy Scouts were down by 26 percent since 1970, while
those for the Red Cross had decreased by 61 percent in the same period.
Even neighborliness was experiencing a slow but steady decline. To be sure,
Putnam continued, these trends were to some degree offset by the growth
of mass-membership groups such as the Sierra Club, the American Association of Retired Persons, and the National Organization of Women. But
these were often coupon-clipping affairs, expecting, if not encouraging,
passive activity from those who paid their dues. Nor did the prevalence of
therapeutic groups such as Alcoholics Anonymous fill the gap. Americans
were, his article concluded, less connected to each other than they previously had been.

Putnam's social scientific research and the social criticism of writers
like William Bennett and other Catholic thinkers establish two different
ways of dealing with the same issue: whether or not America has experienced a significant moral decline. These approaches do overlap.
Putnam could not hide his moral concerns, and Bennett, in his role as co-
chairman of the National Council on Civic Renewal, relied on extensive
social scientific data. Yet there is also little doubt that, in trying to make
its case, its tradition appeals to a different conception of truth.

For Putnam, the issue of whether Americans were somehow less moral resolved itself into an empirical question: if we assume that membership in civic associations is a measurement of moral health, then the proper data, analyzed over time, would reveal to us the state of our moral health. One finds in Putnam's writings no explicitly theological issues raised; "Bowling Alone" is worlds away from St. Augustine or Jonathan Edwards. Putnam's reliance on the concept of social capital—borrowed from economics—implies that the problem in America is one of efficiency, not of morality.[15] Like Francis Fukuyama, Putnam believed that declines in trust made economic and political cooperation more difficult.[16] The tone of his work suggested that, once social science gave us the truth about our condition, we could then take the proper steps to reform society so that it could use its social capital more efficiently.

Contrast Putnam's way of phrasing the problem with that of the authors of the Council on Civic Society's "A Call to Civil Society: Why Democracy Needs Moral Truths," coproduced by the Institute for American Values and the University of Chicago Divinity School. Signed by many intellectuals of diverse faiths—including many of the Catholic intellectuals whose names I invoked earlier—the "Call" begins with Robert Putnam but ends much closer to Jonathan Edwards. One of the questions raised by Putnam's research was why should we care about declining civic participation in the first place. Writing as a political scientist, Putnam, to the degree that he addressed the question at all, answered it by asserting that low civic participation was bad for democracy. But such an answer was no answer, according to the signers of the "Call." Participation is a good only to the degree that it serves some higher purpose. We would not admire active civic organizations if their objective were to promote white supremacy. To call for more democracy, without raising the question of democracy for what, is to leave morality out of the picture entirely.

This the Council on Civic Society was unprepared to do. Different thinkers find different value in civil society, defined as "relations and institutions that are neither created nor controlled by the state." For the council, that value could be found in the capacity of these organizations "to foster competence and character in individuals, build social trust, and help children become good people and good citizens." Active participation in civic life was necessary, not just for the sake of participation itself, but because through socially connected activity "we answer together the most important questions: what is our purpose, what is the right way to act, and what is the common good."

This is strong stuff. For the council was claiming, not only that active participation in the institutions of civil society forces us to ask the right questions, but also that it provides the right answers. As contrary to the times as this way of thinking may be, the authors of the "Call" argued, it was very much along the lines of what the founders believed. In writing a constitution and establishing the framework for a new society, they understood that there were important civic truths to which all Americans ought to be committed, such as the idea that all people were created equal. By themselves, such civic truths "do not tell us how to pursue happiness or how to live a good life." But our founders—as well as those great Americans like Abraham Lincoln and Martin Luther King who followed them— were steeped in biblical and religious sources. When the founders spoke of "laws of nature and of nature's God," or when King made reference to a "higher law," they were expressing the sense that "democracy depends upon moral truths."

Moral truths take on their importance because, timeless as they are, they have their origin in forces—such as nature on the one hand or the realm of the supernatural on the other—that are outside the control of human beings. "Our moral truths underwrite our social well-being primarily because they teach us to govern our appetites and to transcend selfishness," the council claimed. Those who refused to have their appetites held in check—the descendants, so to speak, of Herbert Marcuse—thus live under a moral lie. They fail to realize that freedom does not mean "immunity from restraint." Instead, freedom must be understood as "an ethical condition," as "the morally defined mean between license and slavery." Human beings, the "Call" concluded, are "not autonomous creatures who are the source of their own meaning and perfection." We are rather "intrinsically social beings" who require "connectedness" in order to "approach authentic self-realization." The notion that people can be morally free is a falsehood because if the imperative to work together with others is written in nature or inscribed by God, then those who decide that they would rather go it alone are as misguided as those who insist that water can run uphill or that man can by his own efforts escape his fallen state.

Here, then, we have two important statements about America's moral condition, each appealing to its own conception of truth. Upon which conception—moral truth or empirical truth—ought we to rely? I would like to suggest that there are problems with each, so that the best answer is to appeal to both.

Putnam's appeal to empirical truth turned out to be far more complicated than it may have first seemed to him. His article sparked a veritable cottage industry of critical responses. Some challenged the historical accuracy of Putnam's analysis. Others documented the many ways in which civic participation still took place, especially in the religious dimension of American life.[17] No one devoted as much attention to challenging Putnam's findings as the political scientist Everett Carll Ladd, whose book analyzing where Putnam went wrong came out even before Putnam could turn "Bowling Alone" into a book of his own.[18] Ladd's points were often persuasive. Older civic associations had indeed lost members, Ladd argued, but this was only to be expected. More important was the fact that newer kinds of organizations were gaining members. The decline of Parent Teacher Associations was actually good news for civic engagement, for they were losing members to more activist and engaged Parent Teacher Organizations. There is no evidence that the tendency of Americans to engage in volunteering had diminished. Philanthropy was, if anything, undergoing resurgence. Ladd rejected any notion that Americans ought to engage in moral breast-beating. We have always been a society which prides individualism, he argued. Americans will find a way to respond to their collective needs through their own individualistic inclinations as they always have in the past.

Whether or not Putnam's critics have damaged his case is not a question I need to answer here. My point is rather this: as important as it may be to establish an empirical truth, social science by itself is unlikely ever to resolve our most contentious moral questions. We can generally learn enough about how we behave to rule certain claims out of bounds; for example, no one these days can make a credible case that divorce rates are at historic lows. But the numbers can never command general agreement on the issues so many care most about, such as where our conduct places us in the eyes of God.

Yet as weak a reed as empirical truth may sometimes seem, appeals to moral truth may be even weaker. The authors of the Council on Civil Society's "Call" write as if they know what those moral truths are. But once one tries to apply their ideas more specifically to the possible causes and consequences of America's moral crisis, the certainty behind those truths begins to crumble.

An example of the uncertain quality of what might at first appear to be well-grounded moral truths is the role played by family in contemporary

America. "Self-governance begins with governing the self," wrote the authors of the "Call." "In this sense, the family is the cradle of citizenship, since it is in the family that a child learns, or fails to learn, the essential qualities necessary for governing the self: honesty, trust, loyalty, cooperation, self-restraint, civility, compassion, personal responsibility, and respect for others." In such a way the council endorses an inverted version of the feminist slogan that the personal is the political: we make good families in order to make good citizens. It follows that changes in family life that have made it harder for families to flourish are to a significant degree responsible for the weakening of moral character in America.

Can we say with certainty that this analysis establishes a moral truth that ought to guide how we act in these matters? I think not. There is, for one thing, some discrepant empirical evidence: some of our best citizens—need one again mention Abraham Lincoln and Martin Luther King Jr.—lived in less than ideal families. But an even stronger case is made, if indirectly, by the council itself. The family has indeed faced many challenges that have undermined its capacity to assume responsibility for the moral well-being of children. Yet none of those challenges—violence in the media, increasing materialism, the geographic separation of the three-generation family—is as important as the fact that women have obtained significant autonomy in such areas as the workplace and reproductive rights. If we were to weigh women's rights against the higher moral truth of family solidarity, surely, one would think, we ought to sacrifice the former for the sake of the latter. Yet most women, most men, and most Catholics in America do not respond that way. Indeed, not even the authors of the council's "Call" respond this way, for like many other communitarian critics, they are not willing to take a position so counter to a modern social trend that has been so broad. My point here is not to charge the council with hypocrisy for somehow failing to proclaim its antifeminism, for there is no reason to believe that members of the council were antifeminist. I cite them on this issue rather to illustrate a problem with the idea of relying on moral truths. It is, I believe, an important moral truth that families have great moral responsibilities and cannot be entered into for the sake of the immediate gratification and self-interest of their members. But it is also a great moral truth that all people require a certain autonomy to decide for themselves how their lives are to be led. Each of us chooses between these truths. And that is another way of saying that when they conflict, appeals to some kind of preexisting moral truth simply do not take us very far.

3. Preserving Ambiguity

Both empirical and theological traditions have much to tell us about our current moral state. We would not even be addressing the issue in our society were it not for the alarm raised by social scientists, who, in turn, have presented evidence which clearly indicates the degree to which American society has changed over the past fifty years. But social scientists often cannot put their findings into a context that explains why we ought to care about them. Whether or not one agrees with the Council on Civil Society—and I have made clear my disagreements—its members deserve praise for reminding us that there are matters about which we ought to care deeply. Social science is a form of moral inquiry. But moral inquiry without data fails to persuade. That is why each tradition needs the other.

Yet neither social science nor religiously-grounded social criticism, I believe, has gotten the truth of America's moral tradition correct. And the reason may be that, as different as their two conceptions of truth are, both are too quick to reach it. Putnam's work was hastily over-interpreted, and the sheer volume of the criticism directed against his conclusions ought to cause one to pause before pronouncing that civic America has "disappeared." We need to be reminded, as Michael Schudson often reminds us, that just because things change does not mean that they always become worse.[19] Social scientists, for all their respect for data, are not above the all too human tendency to make dramatic pronouncements. Thus Francis Fukuyama reviews many of the same trends analyzed by Putnam and concludes that America has experienced a "great disruption," while arguing at the same time that we may be witnessing one more historic adjustment in America's social patterns not unlike earlier transformations in its history.[20]

Conservative and communitarian critics of America's moral state are also too quick to rush to judgment. There is, of course, a readily available form of social criticism available to them in the jeremiad. Some—I think here of former Yale Law professor Robert Bork—argue that America at century's end is comparable to Gomorrah, a point of view more sharply drawn than that, for example, of William Bennett.[21] Like William James's religious believers, communitarians come in tough-minded and tender-minded versions, but even the latter—I am thinking here of someone like current Yale Law professor Stephen Carter—barely seem credible when they argue that somehow Americans today are less civil or less motivated by considerations of integrity than they were in the past.[22]

Would each tradition, if given more exposure to the other, benefit? I cannot say for sure. It certainly is possible that apocalyptic social scientists would simply have the worst aspects of their scholarship reinforced by apocalyptic social critics—and vice versa. But in the best of all possible worlds, their mutual interaction would work in a different way. Empirical social science might, from its interaction with religion, come to appreciate the virtue of humility, especially with respect to its theories and methods. A social science that recognized the existence of many religious traditions—and many traditions within each of those traditions—might be less inclined to insist that there is only one path to science. Instead of maintaining that only one approach to knowledge yields valid truth—a sin, in my view, engaged in not only by empirical social scientists, but by Marxists, rational choice theorists, and, in their own way, postmodernists—social scientists would learn from the pluralism of American religion greater respect for pluralism within its own discipline. Were they to do so, their tendency to make grand pronouncements as if they were incontestably true would be replaced by greater appreciation for tentativeness, in many ways the mark of a more mature science.

And were social critics who write under the influence of their religious traditions to interact positively with sociology, they would, I believe, be less likely to speak with the certainty of prophets. Prophetic social criticism exists for prophetic ages and ours, due in part to the emergence of social science, is not one of them—at least not in the way prophets have traditionally spoken. It is not just that one cannot speak as if the vision of the prophet, true for him, must therefore be true for all. It is more that the whole nature of what it means to engage in faith-based persuasion has changed. Were he alive today, Msgr. Ryan could not write books on income distribution or the just wage as if the right position one ought to take on those issues can be deduced from a set of God-given axioms and expect that he will have much of an influence on the general culture. Some would lament that. I would not. For the fact that we live in a pluralistic world— not only that we have competing religions each with its own faith, but that religion has to compete with nonreligious ways of thinking and being over matters that were once the exclusive province of faith—means that prophecy has not so much been eliminated as forced to change its nature. The Catholic perspective on the social question is very much alive, and our society would be a more just one if it paid more attention to that perspective. But it will only pay attention to it to the degree that such a perspective can make its case in ways that appeal to weak believers and even to nonbelievers. Prophecy ought to be more persuasive the less it can take for granted.

Because human beings are meaning-producing creatures whose worlds are both sacred and profane, religion often poses to them questions they desperately need to ask. But because modern human beings require answers that appeal to their reason and not just their sense of awe, social science becomes indispensable to their ways of examining how they live. The great founders of sociology understood this duality. So do contemporary religious traditions. So long as we are the kinds of creatures we are, we can never expect our social science to be reduced to biology, just as we can never expect our religious traditions to be reduced to literature.

Catholicism, like all of America's religious traditions, has asked questions with which sociologists most frequently wrestle. Obviously they do not always answer them the same way; as much as sociology and Catholicism may have overlapped on the social issues, I doubt that the church's position on abortion or gay rights would win much support in sociology departments these days. But we should not allow the differences between Catholicism and sociology—differences that I, for one, hope will never disappear—to allow us to ignore the way they have interacted with each other. And that history suggests that they will continue to interact with each other in the future, not always smoothly and not always directly, but always, it is to be hoped, respectfully.

NOTES

1. John T. McGreevy, "Thinking on One's Own: Catholicism in the American Intellectual Imagination, 1928–1960," *Journal of American History* 84 (1997): 115.

2. Arthur J. Vidich and Stanford M. Lyman, *American Sociology: Worldly Rejections of Religion and Their Directions* (New Haven: Yale University Press, 1985).

3. Cited in McGreevy, "Thinking on One's Own," 116.

4. Ibid., 102.

5. For the latest telling of the story of American Catholicism, see Charles R. Morris, *American Catholic: The Saints and Sinners Who Built America's Most Powerful Church* (New York: Times Books, 1997).

6. William I. Thomas and Florian Znaniecke, *The Polish Peasant in Europe and America* (New York: Dover Publications, 1958). Originally published 1918–1920.

7. James C. Turner, remark made at a meeting of the Lilly Seminar on Religion and Higher Education.

8. Alasdair MacIntyre, *After Virtue: A Study in Moral Theory* (Notre Dame, Ind.: University of Notre Dame Press, 1984), 23.

9. Charles Taylor, *Sources of the Self: The Making of the Modern Identity* (Cambridge: Harvard University Press, 1989).

10. William J. Bennett, John J. DiIulio Jr., and John P. Walters, *Body Count: Moral Poverty—and How to Win America's War against Crime and Drugs* (New York: Simon and Schuster, 1996), and William J. Bennett, *The Book of Virtues: A Treasury of Great Moral Tales* (New York: Simon and Schuster, 1993).

11. Alan Ehrenhalt, *The Lost City: Discovering the Forgotten Virtues of Community in the Chicago of the 1950s* (New York: Basic Books, 1995).

12. Herbert J. Gans, *The Urban Villagers: Group and Class in the Life of Italian-Americans* (Glencoe: Free Press, 1962).

13. Robert Wuthnow, *The Restructuring of American Religion: Society and Faith since World War II* (Princeton: Princeton University Press, 1988); James Davison Hunter, *Culture Wars: The Struggle to Define America* (New York: Basic Books, 1991).

14. Robert Putnam, "Bowling Alone," *Journal of Democracy* 6 (1995): 65–78; see now Robert D. Putnam, *Bowling Alone: The Collapse and Revival of American Community* (New York: Simon and Schuster, 2000).

15. Institute for American Values, "A Call to Civil Society: Why Democracy Needs Moral Truths" (New York: Institute for American Values, 1998).

16. Francis Fukuyama, *Trust: Social Virtues and the Creation of Prosperity* (New York: Free Press, 1995).

17. See, for example, Theda Skocpol and Morris Fiorina, eds., *Civic Engagement in American Democracy* (Washington: Brookings Institution, 1999), and Sidney Verba, Kay Lehman Scholzman, and Henry E. Brady, *Voice and Equality: Civic Voluntarism in American Politics* (Cambridge: Harvard University Press, 1995).

18. Everett Carll Ladd, *The Ladd Report* (New York: Free Press, 1999).

19. Michael Schudson, *The Good Citizen: A History of American Civic Life* (New York: Free Press, 1998).

20. Francis Fukuyama, *The Great Disruption: Human Nature and the Reconstitution of Social Order* (New York: Free Press, 1999).

21. Robert H. Bork, *Slouching toward Gomorrah: Modern Liberalism and American Decline* (New York: ReganBooks, 1996).

22. Stephen L. Carter, *Civility: Manners, Morals, and the Etiquette of Democracy* (New York: Basic Books, 1998), and *Integrity* (New York: Basic Books, 1996).

3

Christian Faith in the Academy

The Role of Physics

JOHN POLKINGHORNE

MY TITLE IS DELIBERATELY AMBIGUOUS, FOR I AM CONCERNED BOTH with the place of Christian faith and thought within the activity of the academic world and also with the trust that I believe the Christian community should place in the truth-seeking work of our universities. Implied by both halves of this concern is the belief that the primary religious question is the question of truth. Christian faith has a place in the academy, not because it has private access to a source of unchallengeable propositions, providing ready-made and nonnegotiable answers to a series of questions about the way things are, but because it preserves and explores certain experiential resources relating to God's interaction with humankind that are of the highest importance and which must be taken into account in a truthful search for comprehensive understanding. Christian thinkers should welcome the opportunities provided by their interaction with the rest of the academy, not because secular learning has some superiority or veto over religious learning, but because those who seek to serve the God of truth must be open to truth from whatever quarter it may come. Moreover, such intercourse may help both the secularist and the believing scholar alike to detect and allow for tricks of perspective that their prior points of view may have imposed upon them.

I recognize that there is a certain degree of optimistic idealism in this agreeable picture and that it assumes a measure of openness and tolerance that neither side has always been disposed to grant to the other. Nevertheless, a fortress mentality, which declines the opportunity for encounter with adherents of a different point of view, is both fatal to enquiry with truthful intent and also the negation of the spirit of the university, rightly understood.

I choose the subject of physics for my example partly, of course, because it was my own discipline in the first half of my career as a university teacher and researcher. It is also a subject that represents in some respects an extreme case. While we may conceive of a Christian philosophy or a Christian sociology, having distinctive characteristics deriving from the insights of the faith, I do not think that we can conceive of anything that could rightly be called a Christian physics. People sometimes ask me how my Christian belief affected my work as a theoretical elementary particle physicist. These enquirers are often believers themselves, and I think they entertain a wistful hope that I shall say that my faith was beneficial in some way to my professional activities. I have to disappoint them. Of course, theoretical physics requires integrity and generosity on the part of its practitioners, but my nonbelieving colleagues equally displayed these characteristics. Where my Christianity does impact upon my understanding of the physical world is when I seek to place my scientific insights within a broader intellectual setting. I shall illustrate this later, when I come to the discussion of certain metaquestions that arise from our scientific experience but which take us beyond science's self-limited power to answer. In other words, it is precisely in the wider setting of the university, rather than within the narrower setting of the physics department, that Christian faith has something to offer to the life of a physicist within the academy.

I am an Anglican priest and so a catholic with a small c, though no less a Catholic for that, I believe. I rejoice to be a member of the universal Christian church and I greatly value that stream within its thought and practice that is commonly called Catholic. I want to hold in balance the insights and resources that are mediated to us through scripture, tradition, and the use of God-given human reason. (We Anglicans like to think of this as our "theological tripod.") I do not want to do all my Christian thinking with the aid of contemporary insights alone, but I wish, as far as I am able, to be in dialogue not only with the foundations of the faith in the first century, but also with the great Christian thinkers of the centuries lying between then and now. I wish to draw on the experience of the whole community of believers, spread out through space and time. Only by these means can we gain release from the intellectual prison house of the present, with all its inherent limitations. There is an important contrast here with science. It is a cumulative subject and the influence of its great figures of the past is sufficiently expressed through the deposit that their contributions make in the sum of contemporary understanding. I can use Newton's ideas on mechanics without ever having to read the *Principia*. On the other hand, theology is intrinsically a diachronic subject. Dialogue with its great thinkers has to continue down through the ages.

I want to see the world as the creation within which the Word was incarnate and within which the sacramental life provides special covenanted experience of the divine presence, mediated through the creaturely gifts of water, bread, and wine. I want to take seriously our created embodiment. Matter matters. A great Anglican thinker of this century, Archbishop William Temple, rightly said that Christianity is the most materialistic of the world religions. These theological concerns sit rather easily with my scientific desire to understand the physical basis of the world in which we live.

Christianity, and perhaps particularly Catholic thinking, rightly recognizes the necessity of community. The lonely vocation of the hermit is seen as being something exceptional. Therefore, to the reality of human embodiment must be added a recognition of the importance of life lived within a society. The church must set a value on institutions and it must encourage their flourishing, including those institutions of higher learning that are called universities. The concept of the community of scholars is a thoroughly Catholic concern. I have the privilege of belonging to an institution that embodies rather explicitly the ideal of a commonwealth of learning, in that major decisions relating to the University of Cambridge are taken in principle, and when necessary in practice, by vote of the Regent House, which is the assembly of the whole university faculty.

I seek to serve the God of truth, and so I believe that there is indeed a truth to be found or, rather, approximated to, since even in science the physical world has a richness that will always elude our total grasp. My belief in God the Creator means that in my encounter with reality I do not fear that I am being deceived by Descartes's malicious demon, nor do I think that I am simply offered an à la carte menu of postmodern postures from which to make my idiosyncratic selection. I am neither a modernist nor a postmodernist, but a critical realist.[1] Here again my religious and my scientific convictions sit easily with each other.

The physical world often surprises us, and it frequently resists the patterns of prior expectation that we seek to impose upon it. Experiences of this kind convince working scientists that they are indeed engaged in theory discovery and not in theory construction—that they attain verisimilitudinous mappings of the physical world that correspond to its reality and are not merely the products of a personally pleasing or complacent agreement to see things this way. Religious experience arises from our encounter with the divine Other, the One whose infinite reality transcends our human finitude and who will never be caught in the puny nets of our rational endeavors. God too repeatedly breaks the bounds of our limited expectation.

I have spent the majority of my working life in the University of Cambridge, an institution founded for the advancement of religion as well as for the advancement of teaching, learning, and research. I think that theology has an indispensable role in a true university, as a reminder that human thinking that neglects the dimension of the transcendent is failing in its task of seeking to embrace the whole of reality.[2] I also think that a university setting is a vital resource for the health of theology, both as a reminder of the paramountcy of the question of truth, and also as affording it contact with those other disciplines of rational enquiry whose insights it must respect and whose achievements will help in theology's endeavor to speak of the One who is the Ground of all. It would not be at all satisfactory if theological study and research were to be confined to seminaries alone. The Catholic emphasis on the value of the natural world, and of natural knowledge, should deliver theologians from the temptation to retreat into some fideistic ghetto. Of course, we need also revelation and grace, but they complete the natural and do not deny or supplant it.

The precise institutional way that the relationship between theology and the rest of the academy is expressed will, naturally, be different according to local circumstances and the history that gave rise to them. The sharp constitutional separation between church and state maintained in the United States is clearly the source of the existence of its many Christian colleges and universities, with their varied confessional bases. If the state educational system is such that theology can only find a place within its institutions of higher learning when it is disguised as the philosophy of religion or as religious studies, then it is understandable that alternative institutions will be established where the subject can be pursued as a self-confessed academic discipline in its own right. This pursuit must be conducted under appropriate conditions of academic freedom, honoring the need to seek truth and understanding where they may be found. It is natural that a Roman Catholic university will wish to give some prominence to teaching the thought of Thomas Aquinas, just as a Lutheran university will do the same for the thought of the great German reformer, but in neither case should there be an institutionalized implication that here can be found all the answers that are needed. Equally, of course, a secular university should not accord prior preference to the skeptical questionings of a David Hume.

In these circumstances, the existence of confessional universities and colleges is seen by many British observers to be a kind of painful necessity in the United States. Such institutions will certainly wish to ensure that their tradition is able to offer its distinctive pastoral care and style of worship on campus, but more open to question, we believe, would be circumstances where this is sustained and emphasized to a degree that results in a great majority of the students being drawn only from one confessional background. Even more questionable would be the prescription of entrance requirements to ensure the existence of such a majority, or the imposition of narrow restrictions on the choice of members of the faculty. The danger being feared here is the imposition of a narrowness of experience and understanding that could militate against the openness of thought in the quest for truth that is part of the heritage of a university.

I can see that British Anglicans might seem pretty vulnerable to riposte if they make such comments. After all, did we not retain a stranglehold on Oxford and Cambridge until late in the nineteenth century? Indeed we did, but these universities have benefited greatly (not least in theology) by its abolition. Do not the British still maintain denominational secondary schools, many of them with an Anglican basis? Indeed we do, and I think this can be defended at the relevant age levels, though the consequences of a separated educational system in Northern Ireland give one pause about this. We believe, however, that university students have reached a stage of maturity where the confessional solidarity of their peers is no longer to be regarded as needed or desirable in order to provide encouragement to their own Christian faith. Supposing the contrary seems to be acting in a way that is overprotective. One might well assign greater value to a faith that is strengthened through exchanges with those of a contrary opinion. I make these comments not because of a claim to superiority on the part of the British system, but simply as as an indication of how aspects of the North American scene can be perceived from a different perspective.

My remarks so far have been very general, and as an exploration of what they might actually mean I want to go on to consider how physics may find a place within an intellectual tradition informed by Catholic principles, and how the idea of a university can and should embrace both natural science and theology in harmonious dialogue. Of course, physics enjoys a proper autonomy within its own limited domain. Physical questions will receive physical answers given for physical reasons. To suppose the contrary would be to fall into the grievous error of the God of the gaps, a pseudo-deity functioning as the "explanation" of last resort when contemporary science had not yet attained an answer on its own terms. Attempting to trade on temporary scientific ignorance not only produced a "god" who faded away with the continuing advance of knowledge, but it also represented a serious theological mistake. The Creator is the God of the whole universe, and not just a deity lurking in its murkier corners.

Yet, if there is a fundamental unity of knowledge—a belief underwritten by faith in the unity of the Creator—then we may expect there to be family likenesses between different enquiries into reality, and also a degree of incompleteness in the intellectual satisfaction that any discipline can give from within its own resources alone. It has been a common theme in the writings of scientist-theologians, such as Ian Barbour, Arthur Peacocke, and myself, to detect a measure of comradely relationship between the programs of science and of theology as each pursues the shared goal of truthful understanding attained through motivated belief.[3] Of course, there are differences, arising principally from the very different subject matters of the two disciplines. Human beings transcend the physical world, and so we can put it to the test, giving to science its secret weapon of the experimental method. Theology is concerned with the divine Reality who transcends our finite selves and who is to be met with in awe and obedience. "You shall not put the lord your God to the test" is just a fundamental fact of the spiritual life. In the transpersonal realm of encounter with the divine, just as in the interpersonal realm of human mutual encounter, testing has to give way to trusting as the appropriate medium of engagement.

The form of connection that we may expect between science and theology is that "limit questions" will arise within the former that carry us beyond its borders and point us to the necessity of finding a more comprehensive account into which they can be integrated. Theology relates to this wider quest because it operates not only as a first-order discipline like science, having its own domain of primary experience that it seeks to understand (systematic theology), but also as the second-order discipline of theistic metaphysics (philosophical theology), in which theology seeks to set the insights of all the first-order disciplines within the comprehensive matrix of understanding that is afforded by belief in God as the Creator of the whole of reality. The considerations that follow are intended to indicate how, in such a scheme, physics can find its appropriate place within the the wider intellectual context of the whole university and within the truthseeking community of the church.

First, fundamental physics speaks of a world of great rational transparency and great rational beauty. Mathematics is its prime descriptive tool and the search for beautiful equations has proved an immensely powerful guide to discovery. Both Albert Einstein and Paul Dirac were masters of this heuristic art. Eugene Wigner described mathematics' amazing power to unlock the secrets of the universe as being an "unreasonable effectiveness," a gift that we neither deserve nor understand. The deep intelligibility of the universe induces in the scientist a sense of wonder, which is one of the principal rewards for all the weary labor necessarily involved in scientific research. Neither the vastness of cosmic space nor the intimate structure of nuclear matter—the one 10^{23} larger than the scale of the everyday, the other 10^{-18} smaller—has proved inaccessible to human understanding, despite their counterintuitive characters when compared with mundane thinking. Physicists rejoice that this is so, but physics itself cannot explain our good fortune in this respect. What appears at the scientific level to be just an incredibly happy accident, becomes intelligible at the theological level as the encounter of creatures made in the image of God with the rational created order, truly expressive of the Mind of its Creator. Here we see already how both science and theology intertwine in that search for understanding which is the prime task of the university, and how theology can play an overarching and integrating role, complementing science but not pretending to be able to tell it what to think in its own domain.

It would be an act of intolerable intellectual laziness not to attempt to comprehend why our quest for understanding is, in fact, so fruitful, why physical reality is so perfectly and satisfyingly intelligible. The Catholic tradition of Thomist thought has always testified that the search for truth and understanding, if pursued wholeheartedly and without reservation, will prove ultimately to be the search for God, whether initially named by name or not. This insight was given luminous expression in the writings of Bernard Lonergan, for whom "God is the all-sufficient explanation, the eternal rapture glimpsed in every Archimedean cry of Eureka." [4] That sentence could serve as an epigraph for a university informed by Catholic principles.

Second, physics is characterized by a drive toward unification. Galileo abolished the Aristotelian distinction between terrestial physics and celestial physics. The nineteenth century saw the combination of electric and magnetic phenomena into the single account of electromagnetism, attained through the deep insight of James Clerk Maxwell (himself a deeply Christian man). Today, the Holy Grail of particle physics is the elusive Grand Unified Theory, thought to be capable of synthesizing all the basic forces of nature into a comprehensive whole. It has not yet been discovered, despite much effort, but, we may ask, what is the source of the instinctive belief of physicists that such a goal should eventually prove within our grasp? It derives from a deep trust in the integrated rational structure of the universe. The theologian will see this act of faith as another intuition of the trustworthiness of the One God who is the sole origin of created reality. Once again, we may expect that there is a truth to be found, so that scrupulous and honest enquiry will bring the reward of discovery. The activity of science, and indeed of all rational investigation, is based upon the belief that we live in a world that ultimately will be found to be a cosmos, a universe that makes total sense.

Third, even within physics itself, we can see that reality takes different forms according to the nature of the entities being met with. Notoriously, Heisenberg's uncertainty principle limits our access to the details of quantum process. The kind of clear and picturable story that we can tell about the everyday world of Newtonian physics is unavailable to us in that quantum regime. If the quantum world is to be known, it must be known on its own terms, in its cloudiness and probabilistic fitfulness. In other words, there is no general epistemology. The unity of knowledge is more subtle than being simply the result of employing a flat and ready-made universal epistemological technique. Nevertheless, once we accept the need to conform our search for knowledge to the nature of the object of knowledge, we seem in physics to be able to gain that knowledge. The quantum world is counterintuitive, but it is not intellectually opaque to us. Once again, mathematics proves to be an indispensable guide in shaping our thoughts, though I must confess that currently there remain significant unresolved problems about how the formalism of quantum theory is to be interpreted in directly physical terms.

The often-recounted tale of the nature of light illustrates these points with particular force and clarity. Perhaps the greatest achievement of nineteenth-century physics was the establishment of the nature of light as waves of electromagnetic energy. Yet, in the opening years of the twentieth century, the researches of Max Planck and Albert Einstein made it equally clear that there are circumstamces in which light unquestionably behaves as if it were composed of particles. Since a wave is spread out and oscillating, and particles are like little bullets, the physicists seemed to be faced with an intolerably paradoxical situation. No progress would have been made by attempting recourse to oversimplification by sweeping either the wave or the particle evidence under the carpet. For a while, all that could be done was to hold on to experience by the skin of one's intellectual teeth, however contradictory the situation seemed to be. The story has a happy ending, for such intellectual fortitude was eventually rewarded. With the discovery of the modern version of quantum theory, and particularly quantum field theory, the dilemma was resolved in a rationally coherent fashion. A field is spread out (and so wavelike), but when it is quantized its energy comes in countable packets (which is particle-like behavior).

If these kinds of epistemological considerations hold within physics, how much more may this be expected to be true of the other disciplines of the university. Their variety, with each practicing its proper mode of rational enquiry, provides, in principle, the ideal setting in which to recognize the diversity of the ways in which knowledge may be gained. The university is the institutional embodiment of the necessity for multiple perspectives upon the many levels of reality encountered in the world. This variety does not imply the fragmentation of knowledge but, rather, the richness of the real. I sometimes feel anxious that respect for the achievements of science will hinder other disciplines in holding fast to the idiosyncratic methods proper to their own enquiries. "Physics envy" is a bad epistemological condition from which to suffer and one might fear one saw signs of it when, for instance, New Testament scholars seem tempted to invent quasi-algorithmic approaches to the assessment of their material. They invent rules of "reliability" such as double dissimilarity (attributing a saying to Jesus if it has no parallels in either first-century Judaism or in the thought of the early church) or multiple attestation (independently present in several sources). Of course, these factors are of some significance, but it seems to me that New Testament critics need to use methods that are more subtle and discerning than simply resorting to an undue reliance on this kind of almost mechanical approach. For example, in relation to the criterion of double dissimilarity, it really is very odd not to recognize that Jesus must have both derived much from his Jewish inheritance and also greatly influenced the thinking of his post-resurrection followers.

We live in a cosmos that is many-layered. The hierarchies of the sciences reflect something of that plenitude, with the levels of matter, life, consciousness, and society calling for the insights of physics and chemistry, biology, psychology, and social science. Further aspects of the richness of reality are indicated by the humane dimensions of the moral, the aesthetic, and the religious. The concerns of the university should relate to all these multiple modes of engagement with reality, and the proper autonomy of its academic faculties and departments reflects the irreducibility and conceptual independence of each of these levels of human encounter and enquiry. Biology is not merely physics writ large, nor are the concerns of ethics, aesthetics, and theology mere epiphenomenal manifestations of something more prosaic and banal. Each discipline has its own value; there is no master discipline to which all the rest must submit.

Yet, the increasing specialization of modern knowledge, and the increasingly frenetic competitiveness with which it is pursued, militate against the maintenance of the university as a true community of learning. There is a pressing need to witness to this ideal and to give it support before it is lost. Otherwise the prevailing tendency to force scholars into a narrow focus, knowing more and more about less and less, will be pushed to the vanishing point.

Universities must be catholic in the nonecclesial sense of the word, concerned with the whole. They should also be centers where interdisciplinary study is particularly encouraged and cherished. For many years now, I have been a contributor to the growing dialogue between science and theology. I am conscious of the risks involved when one moves out of the safety of one's narrow professional field—in my case, theoretical elementary particle physics—and attempts to engage with other disciplines, such as theology, in which one may have a deep interest but no claim to expert knowledge of the kind that can only come from many years of apprenticeship and journeyman work in the subject. I am also conscious of the rewards of enhanced understanding that this precarious interdisciplinary activity can give. We have to be prepared to stick our necks out if we are to be able to see very far.

Who can doubt that the doctrine of creation has been enriched by science's discovery that the universe has had a long evolutionary history? Instead of a God who brings all into being ready-made, with a snap of the divine fingers, we are now offered the theologically more profound picture of the God of love who endows creation with an inbuilt potentiality and then allows it (in Charles Kingsley's splendid phrase, coined very soon after the publication of *The Origin of Species*) "to make itself." Moreover, through this insight, science affords theology some modest but real help with the most profound and perplexing of all its problems, namely that of theodicy, the search for an understanding of why there is so much suffering in a world claimed to be the creation of a loving and powerful God. The evolution of life has been driven by the biochemical processes of genetic mutation in cells, the source of the coming to be of new kinds of living beings. But exactly the same kinds of biochemical processes must also allow other cells to mutate and become malignant. One cannot have the one without the other. That there is cancer in the world is not due to the callousness or incompetence of the Creator; it is the necessary cost of the good of a world allowed to make itself. As science advances, it discovers more and more of the interrelatedness of the processes of the universe. It proves to be a kind of package deal, and the feelings that we often have that the Creator should have done better by retaining the good and eliminating the bad in creation as we experience it, are likely to be false.

Theology is well aware of the dangers of a narrow and imperialistic epistemology. Its thought about how God is known must always strive to conform to the way in which God has actually chosen to reveal the divine nature. This has been a particular theme in the writings of those in the Barthian tradition, such as the Reformed theologian Thomas Torrance.[5] Remarkably, that theophany has centered on the vulnerability and ambiguity of a human life, a Word written not on stone but in flesh. Theology knows that it must guard itself against turning any of its images of God into an unrevisable idol. The warnings of an apophatic theology to respect the ultimate mystery of God must be heeded, though not to the point of a total paralysis of theological utterance. I suppose that those of us who, in one way or another, are the heirs of the rationally confident Latin church of the West, need to pay particular attention to that warning. We may recall that Augustine, the Father whose thinking has influenced so many streams of theological thought in the West, knew that he could not speak adequately of the mystery of the Holy Trinity but nevertheless thought, surely rightly, that it was better to say something than to remain in total silence.

Fourth, physics has learnt that the world is full of surprises and that the common sense of everyday cannot be the measure of everything. The instinct of the physicist is not to ask, "Is it reasonable?" as if somehow we knew beforehand what are to be the criteria of rationality in some new domain of experience, but rather, "What makes you think this might be the case?" That, of course, is an altogether more open question. Sometimes revisions may be called for of a most surprising kind.

The nature of the quantum world, for example, is such that it obeys its own kind of logic. An electron can not only be in a state of being "here" or in a state of being "there," but it can also be in a state which is a mixture (a superposition) of these possibilities.[6] The difference between classical physics and quantum physics derives precisely from this fact that what are immiscible possibilities in the former can be combined in the latter. The resulting unpicturable state constitutes a middle term of a kind undreamed of by Aristotle. In consequence, in the quantum world the distributive law of classical logic does not hold. If we have to revise our modes of thought so radically in order to encompass the realm of subatomic reality, it would not be surprising if a similar requirement proved necessary in our thought about divine reality.

Physicists are what I like to call "bottom-up thinkers," seeking to move from experience to understanding, and wary of self-evident general principles, because so often they have proved, on further investigation, to be neither evident nor general.[7] I believe that theology can also be done in this style, provided a suitably generous concept of acceptable motivating evidence is allowed. This last proviso is essential if theology is to be granted its due intellectual autonomy, for it cannot be subjected to a demand that its experience and argumentation should accord with the requirements of some basically atheistic protocol.

Fifth, physics derives much of its power from its ability to use the experimental method. This in turn depends upon the repeatability of physical experience, which itself derives partly from a degree of separability present in the physical world. The latter means that physical process can be split up into separate pieces, each capable of being considered on its own. (In fact, we shall see later that there are limits to this atomistic methodology, despite its having proved so effective as science has progressed by decomposing entities into their constituent parts, whose behavior could then be understood more simply. We are discovering that there is more interconnectedness present in the physical world than had previously been appreciated. Science is beginning to recover a greater understanding of the need to think in terms of wholes as well as parts.)

Separability, when it holds, implies that, to a sufficiently good approximation, there are situations in which what is happening here is independent of what is happening elsewhere. In that case, the same local arrangement repeats the previous situation. (If this were not so, science would never have been able to get started, for then one would have had to understand everything before one could understand anything.) The resulting property of repeatability implies, in principle, a degree of universal access to knowledge. If you doubt the result of my experiment, you can try it for yourself. Of course, this is very much an "in principle" statement. If my experiment involved the use of a high energy particle accelerator, you are unlikely to have either the expertise or the access to a facility that would permit this confirmation. Nevertheless, there is at least the possibility of professional cross-checking, and in physics this leads to intersubjective confidence and agreement about results. The other side of the coin, however, is that physicists are temperamentally disinclined to recognize the significance of the unique. They feel this even in respect of the role of the great geniuses whose discoveries have furthered the advance of scientific knowledge. None is indispensable. Einstein discovered general relativity, the beautiful modern theory of gravity. It came into his mind fully-fledged, solely through his own insightful endeavor, pursued over a period of eight years. However, had he not made this great discovery, the theory would eventually have come to light, even if it did so later on and as the piecemeal result of the labor of several scientists of lower calibre. By contrast, in the realm of artistic creativity, the role of the unique individual is absolutely indispensable. Only Dante could have written the *Divine Comedy*; only Beethoven could have composed the late quartets. What is true of the geniuses is true of all in the arts, in lesser ways. We never hear one of those Beethoven quartets the same way twice, even if we play the same disc.

Suspicion of the unique is a crippling disadvantage in relation to any attempt to engage reality at the levels of personal and transpersonal experience, where repetition is not conceivable. In the realm of the personal, testing has to give way to trusting as the basis of true encounter; the unique must be recognized and valued for what it is; the individual has an indispensable role to play.

Contact with university colleagues in the humanities will serve to remind the physicist of the unacceptable narrowness of an undue preference for the repeatable. Everyday life will do the same, since physicists are persons as well as scientists. Some corrective is even available from within physics itself. There have been unique physical regimes of great significance that are beyond our powers ever to recreate. If the search for a Grand Unified Theory eventually comes to fruition, the only regime in which many of its characteristic consequences would have been directly manifested would be at ultrahigh energies, many orders of magnitude beyond laboratory possibility, which only existed in the unique circumstances of the very early universe.

The role for the unique is even clearer in a historical science such as biology. The particular and contingent deposits of terrestrial evolution play an important part in understanding the nature of contemporary organisms. In contrast, physics is largely an atemporal subject, for its basic laws are always the same. It is only at this rather flat level of reality at which physics operates that it is relatively easy to lose sight of the significance of the unique.

Sixth, and related to the previous point, there is an inclination on the part of the physicist to overvalue the general in relation to the particular. The discovery commonly called the Anthropic Principle that the laws of nature as we experience them in our universe are "finely tuned" to the possibility of carbon-based life, came as a great shock to many physicists.[8] It turned out that a star like our Sun has only been able to shine steadily for billions of years, fueling the development of life on earth, because of a process that is controlled by a delicate balance between the intrinsic strengths of gravity and electromagnetism. If gravity were only three times stronger than it is, the stars would burn so fiercely that they would die out within millions of years, far too short a period to permit life to develop on any planets that might encircle them. To take another example, the chemical raw materials of life, such as carbon, are made in the interior nuclear furnaces of the stars through an exquisitely balanced chain of processes. If the nuclear forces had been any different from what they actually are in our universe, links in this chain would have been broken and the evolution of life would have been an impossibility. We are all made of stardust and without the right kind of stardust around, a universe is condemned to a history of boring sterility. To many these particularities of the physical fabric of the universe were an unpleasant shock, implying that there was something very special about our cosmos and running counter to the instinctive expectation that it would just be a typical specimen, so to speak, with nothing uniquely significant about it. Consequently, some have been driven to the uneconomic metaphysical speculation that there is a vast portfolio of different universes—a general collection of actually existing possible worlds—in which our particular one is then anthropically fruitful simply "by chance." One cannot help thinking that so prodigal a proposal is a rather desperate strategy to avoid a theistic conclusion. Theology, of course, has no difficulty in offering a much more economic explanation of fine tuning, for it does not suppose the universe to be just "any old world," but rather a creation that has been endowed by its Creator with those laws and circumstances that have enabled it to have a fruitful history.

Participation in the intellectual community of the university will provide physicists with a corrective to this particular "calling's snare" (to use a phrase from a Charles Wesley hymn). If rationality is the attempt to conform thinking to the nature of the object of thought, as I believe it to be, there must be an irreducible role, in the encounter with personal and transpersonal reality, for the scandal of the particular. Of course, acceptance of this fact is central to the possibility of an adequate Christology. Jesus Christ cannot be pigeonholed under some general rubric of holy man or wandering prophet.

I believe that theism only attains a commanding credibility when it is expounded in its Trinitarian fullness. This assertion runs counter to the commonly held view that a pallid deism, with its God who amounts to no more than the abstract figure of the Cosmic Architect, is somehow a more credible kind of belief, because it makes so little demand upon our intellectual acceptance. I think this is a mistake. The God of deism does so little work that, as history illustrates, this minimal deity is always in danger of fading away into nothingness. When we consider cosmic history, the emergence of self-conscious beings on earth seems the most surprising and significant development that we know about. In ourselves and in our hominid ancestors, the universe became aware of itself. As Pascal said, human beings are small and insubstantial on the cosmic scale—mere reeds—but we are thinking reeds, and so greater than all the stars, for we know them and ourselves and they know nothing. If the emergence of the personal has been so significant a cosmic event, it is more than likely that a fully personal God (using the word in some stretched and analogical sense) is the Creator of this universe, a deity much richer in divine character than the abstraction of the deistic Great Mathematician.

A physicist expects a fundamental theory to be coherent in a simplicity that supports a rich complexity, profound in the novel illumination it affords, and often surprising in its initial counterintuitiveness. These characteristics have been present in all major advances in our understanding of the physical world; they can be expected to be present in Catholic theology also. Belief in the Father as the Fount of being, in the Son as the divinely uttered Word manifested in the flesh, in the Spirit poured out on humanity, and in their essential unity in the one divine nature, has about it a profundity that a physicist ought to be able to recognize and respond to. It is a deeply exciting idea that the mysterious and unimaginable God has acted to make the divine nature known in the plainest possible way by living the life of a man in Jesus Christ. It is a profoundly moving idea that the God who brought into being this strange world, with all its pain and suffering, is not just a compassionate spectator from the outside of the bitterness present within its history, but in the cross of Christ has stretched out to embrace and accept its suffering from the inside. The Christian God is the Crucified God, truly the fellow sufferer who understands.[9]

Trinitarian theology bids fair to be the true Theory of Everything (to use the phrase employed by some particle physicists as an overblown claim about what they might hope to find in their little corner of reality). In Christian theology's concept of the work of creation, the different levels of human experience, which otherwise seem so puzzlingly independent of each other, are drawn together into an intelligible unity. Our scientific experience of the rational order of the world is a reflection of the Mind of the Creator; our ethical intuitions are intimations of the divine will; our aesthetic experiences are a sharing in God's joy in creation; our religious experiences are indeed responses to the gracious presence of the divine.

It is an extremely important task to present the Catholic faith to the academy, set forth in all its rich coherence, calling on the resources of a motivated belief, and presenting the argument in as honest and scrupulous a fashion as possible. I sometimes fear that contemporary theology will not prove equal to this calling. It is threatened by two temptations that could prove to be disastrous losses of theological nerve. One is the retreat into the fideistic ghetto, by opting out of open discussion within the university and subsiding into a cozy conversation conducted within an enclave of like-minded people. When one thinks of the great figures of our shared Catholic tradition—people like Augustine and Aquinas (great heroes of mine), who combined the deepest spirituality with the highest intellectual power and integrity—one sees what a betrayal this would be. The servants of the God of truth must always have the highest respect for truth, from wherever that truth may come.

The countertemptation would be to seek too ready an accommodation with what society will find easy to assimilate. It may be less demanding to think of Jesus as some kind of inspired and inspiring "new emergent," illustrating a new possibility for human living, but that is simply inadequate to the phenomenon of Christ, as recorded in the New Testament and witnessed to by the church. The Christian community's experiences of prayer and its intuitions of providence cannot, without violating their character, be reduced to accounts of internal psychological attitudes. Interesting enough, some of my unbelieving scientific friends find this lowest common denominator approach to religious belief as unsatisfactory as I do. They see that if there is any truth in religion, it will not be at the level of banality.

Seventh, I am sorry to say that some physicists think of their subject as being absolutely fundamental, with everything else either a corollary from it or mere opinion. It is hard to overestimate the crassness of this position, depending as it does on an unwarranted imperialist reductionism, and regarding ultimate reality as simply the interchange of energy between constituents. The rest of the academy must rightly protest against this preposterous claim, and even within physics itself it will be hotly contested. Those who study turbulent fluids are not disposed to consider their phenomena as simply corollaries to the theory of quarks. Higher-level concepts are required that cannot be reduced to statements about constituents. Once we move on to consider wider human experience, the implausibility of a reductionist account becomes even more evident. Music is very much more than neural response to vibrations in the air. What is the real character of that mysterious and powerful encounter with reality that is afforded to us by listening to Bach's *Mass in B Minor* is beyond science's ability to explain. Music poses an important test of adequacy for any metaphysical scheme that may be proposed.

Reductionism is an intellectually suicidal strategy. The view that thought is no more than the multiple excitation of neurons subverts the very nature of rationality, for what would guarantee the validity of the outputs of such a purely physical process? In the end, reductionists always saw off the branch on which they seek to sit. All tacitly invoke a saving clause in favor of their own endeavors, assuming that they are not to be brought down with everything else to the level of meaningless process.

From within physical science itself, a number of insights are emerging that serve to restore a balance between talk of parts and talk of the whole. The study of complex systems is at present in its infancy, and heavily dependent upon computer modeling, but it is already showing up phenomena in which there is the spontaneous generation of astonishing degrees of overall orderly patterned behavior. For example, Stuart Kauffman considered a network whose physical analogue would be an array of lightbulbs, each of whose behavior (off or on) was correlated with the state of two other bulbs in the network.[10] If there are 10,000 bulbs in the array, there are about 103,000 different states in which, in principle, this kind of correlation might occur. Yet, an array started off from a randomly selected initial configuration soon settles down to cycling through not more than about one hundred states of specific illumination. This represents the generation of a staggering degree of structural order in the behavior of the bulbs making up the total array. It is becoming clear that complex systems require for adequate discussion not only the bits and pieces account of traditional thinking about exchanges of energy, but also a holistic causal concept that one might call "active information."[11] ("Information" because it is concerned with pattern; "active" because it is concerned with what actually brings about novel states of affairs.)

These kinds of holistic tendencies turn out to be quite widespread. The theory of chaos deals with systems that are so sensitive to circumstances that they are never truly isolatable from the effects of their environment, implying that they cannot be treated satisfactorily in a separable way.[12] Most surprising of all, perhaps, the so-called EPR effect shows that, even at the microscopic level of the quantum world, there is an irreducible degree of long-range togetherness and mutual entanglement.[13] Once two quantum entities have interacted with each other, they retain a power of instantaneous mutual influence upon each other. An observation performed on one will have an immediate causal effect on the other, however far apart they may have separated. Even the subatomic world, it seems, cannot be treated atomistically.

Eighth, as science advances it confers power through its vigorous offspring, technology. Ernest Rutherford's researches early in the twentieth century into the nature of the atom led eventually to the possibility of nuclear weapons and nuclear power. This was quite contrary to what he had expected, for Rutherford died in 1937 believing that his discoveries would never have practical consequences. At present, genetics is advancing at an astonishing rate, giving us the ambiguous power to intervene in DNA, the thread of life itself. All such discoveries present new options for humanity, some of which will be beneficial and some of which will be malign. If we are to use these new developments aright, to choose the good and refuse the bad, we shall have to add wisdom to the knowledge that science has given us. But where is wisdom to be found? Certainly not solely within the scientific community, though it will also not be found without that community's assistance, for only the experts can assess what are the possibilities inherent in a new discovery and what their consequences might prove to be. Certainly not only within the university, though disciplines such as moral philosophy have a role to play and the opportunities provided by the academy for interdisciplinary dialogue will be valuable.

I have served on several British government committees concerned with making recommendations about the ethical application of scientific research. These have been concerned with developments in fields, such as genetics, that are far removed from my personal scientific expertise in elementary particle physics. In our deliberations we had first to listen carefully to the professional evidence presented to us, and our expert colleagues on the committee played important parts in helping us to do this. When we came to framing our recommendations, however, we were no longer a mixed committee of experts and nonexperts, but a single body of persons, seeking together to find where the common good would lie.

In that search, we need as much help as we can acquire. The great religious traditions are reservoirs of wise thinking about ethical issues. Though they cannot claim a monopoly on moral insight, their contributions will be indispensable in the attempt to reach wise decisions about what may be done and what may not be done.

Physicists and other scientific workers are members of society, and they cannot claim to be isolated moral atoms, bearing no responsibility for the subsequent use of their discoveries. Neither, of course, can they be made judges in their own cause. Not everything that can be done, should be done. The persistent temptation in scientific research is to get carried away with the excitement of it all, and so to do the next thing almost unthinkingly and without reflection on what might ethically be involved in doing so. Society as a whole has to say to science, "Have you really thought about what it is that you are doing and where it is going?" We shall not find our way in these matters if there is not extensive interaction and discussion between all the participating parties. One of the depressing features of much contemporary ethical debate is that it so often takes the form of the clash of single-issue pressure groups. One side asserts that the new development is the best thing ever; we cannot have too much of it. The other side asserts that it is the worst thing ever; we should have nothing to do with it. It is very unlikely that either side is right. We need temperate debate in which people of goodwill, bringing to the table different insights and perspectives, work together in the difficult but essential task of sifting the good from the bad.

Universities are well placed to encourage and sponsor this dialogue. So also is the church, given the breadth of experience of its members, and I would dearly like to see it doing much more to create meeting places in which there can be calm, truth-seeking discussion of the perplexities that face us, conducted between people of ethical goodwill and integrity of purpose. Of course, if the church is to do this, it cannot come to the common table with all the answers already up its sleeve. It must be prepared for true dialogue.

I think that the universities, at their best, offer vital opportunities both for the physicist and for the theologian. The physicist can be helped to see that subject's embeddedness within a much wider human quest for truth and understanding. The theologian can learn from the scientist what the pattern and history of creation have actually been like. In turn, theology can seek to show how Christian faith is deeply concerned with questions of truth and has reasonable motivation for its beliefs, which are not proffered on the sole basis of authoritative assertion. Together, the physicist and the theologian can affirm their common belief in the unity and value of knowledge. The Christian defense of that value is not framed in terms of a pragmatic strategy of utilitarian usefulness, but it derives from a respect for the worth of created reality. The Christian trust in the unity of knowledge rests on belief in the One God who is the Creator of all. The Catholic faith does not invite us to an act of intellectual suicide, as if we had to shut our eyes and believe impossible things simply on someone's say so, but, on the contrary, it offers us the prospect of the most comprehensive and satisfying knowledge of reality. That is why it has an important contribution to make to our institutions of higher learning.

NOTES

1. John Polkinghorne, *Beyond Science* (Cambridge: Cambridge University Press, 1996), chapters 2, 5.

2. John Polkinghorne, *Science, Faith, and Understanding* (New Haven: Yale University Press, 2000), chapter 1.

3. John Polkinghorne, *Scientists as Theologians* (London: SPCK, 1996), chapter 2.

4. Bernard Longeran, *Insight* (London: Darton, Longman and Todd, 1958), 684.

5. Thomas Torrance, *Theological Science* (Oxford: Oxford University Press, 1969).

6. John Polkinghorne, *The Quantum World* (Princeton: Princeton University Press, 1984), chapter 3.

7. John Polkinghorne, *The Faith of a Physicist* (Princeton: Princeton University Press, 1994), and *Science and Christian Belief* (London: SPCK, 1994).

8. John Barrow and Frank Tipler, *The Anthropic Cosmological Principle* (Oxford: Oxford University Press, 1986).

9. Jurgen Moltmann, *The Crucified God* (London: SCM Press, 1974).

10. Stuart Kauffman, *At Home in the Universe* (Oxford: Oxford University Press, 1995).

11. John Polkinghorne, *Belief in God in an Age of Science* (New Haven: Yale University Press, 1998), chapter 3.

12. James Gleick, *Chaos* (London: Heinemann, 1998).

13. Polkinghorne, *The Quantum World.*

4

Not All the Nations Furiously Rage Together

BRUCE RUSSETT

1. Perspectives on Peace and War

For any observer of international relations, the world as we experience it is full of testimony to sinful human nature, in this now-passing century no less than in others. Governments oppress their own people and commit aggression against their neighbors. World politics is conducted in a condition of anarchy. "Anarchy" is meant in the sense of its Greek source, not as "chaos" but as "without a ruler," with no overarching authority to enforce order. There is some order, but in a world far from ready for a global government, such order as exists is not substantially the product of hierarchical imposition.

Realist theorists of international relations say that in such a condition each country is potentially an enemy of every other—intentionally or not, each is a threat to the others' security and very existence. This tradition, like the anarchy which underlies it, has a long history from Thucydides, Machiavelli, and Hobbes and shaped the perspective of theologians like Reinhold Niebuhr. Many Catholic analysts share it. The so-called Westphalian system—dated from the 1648 treaty of Westphalia but already visible from the peace of Augsburg in the previous century—has been called an example of a kind of original sin. Rulers, by throwing off any remaining superordinate authority, affirmed their sovereign autonomy, and in so doing accepted a system whereby that autonomy would always be at risk from acquisitive designs by their fellows. Realists see international relations, in the absence of imposition of authority by a world state, as caught forever in this precarious state of "freedom."

The possibility of violence is always present. For this reason, and on the principle of the right of collective self-defense, the Christian tradition of nonviolence has had little impact on the behavior of nations. Rather, much of the Christian tradition has been devoted to efforts to mitigate the exercise of violence by normative strictures. It was expressed in the Truce of God and Peace of God movements of the Middle Ages, and in the principles of the just war tradition from St. Augustine to the present. These efforts have often been derided, but their effects have not been trivial. The just war tradition lives, providing some still very imperfect restraints on when and how nations conduct wars. It is a modified form of realism, which accepts that nations may sometimes go to war. The just war principles, like any other set of norms, are subject to differing interpretations and can be twisted in the service of realpolitik. Those of us who have tried to develop and apply them to actual situations know how readily our intellectual constructs can be put to purposes of which we disapprove, much as nuclear physicists recoiled from the uses to which their creation was put.[1]

Yet there are other kinds of restraints on the use of force in international politics. States do not fight all others at all times even when purely realist principles dominate; they are constrained by geography, the balance of power, and the coincidence of national interests expressed in alliances. In the realist system, deterrence forms the heart of survival. Deterrence, however, really is a miserable way of avoiding war, and a miserable way to live. To treat all international politics as unending struggle, and everyone as a potential enemy, risks becoming less an adaptation to reality than a creator of reality, a self-fulfilling prophecy. If it were simply an inaccurate depiction of reality, it would be a poor guide to practical action. To the degree it becomes a self-fulfilling prophecy, it is also immoral.

A competing perspective on international politics is less bleak, and deserves equal or greater attention from Christians concerned to limit the resort to violence. This perspective, now sometimes labeled liberal-institutionalist, is associated with such classical analysts as Locke, Grotius, and Kant. Just over two hundred years ago, Kant suggested that "republican constitutions," a "commercial spirit" of international trade, and a lawful federation of interdependent republics would provide the basis for sustained peace. The alternative (even more imaginable in our nuclear era) would be peace of a different sort: "a vast grave where all the horrors of violence and those responsible for them would be buried."[2] Consequently Kant argued that there was a duty to work for peaceful international relations. Because Kant believed that natural processes of self-interest impelled individuals to act in ways that virtually guarantee a just peace, that peace was not simply an ideal to him. Kant was also realistic in acknowledging that nations must act prudently until the federation of interdependent republics is established.

Often the realist and Kantian perspectives are characterized as antithetical. That is an error. Kant affirmed much of realist theory, incorporating it yet regarding it as incomplete. Both perspectives view conflict and the threat of violence as inherent in an anarchic world. While Kant accepted Hobbes's description of conflict among many of the nations, he went far beyond it. He was convinced that within a "federation" of liberal republics a genuine peace could be developed. This positive peace would rest more on the three Kantian supports—representative government, commercial exchange embodied in "cosmopolitan law," and a system of international law among republics governed domestically by the rule of law—than on power politics. The pacific federation Kant envisioned is not a world state. Its members remain sovereign, linked only by confederational or collective security arrangements. The difference between the two traditions is that he sees democratic governance, economic interdependence, and international law (and organizations) as means to supersede the security dilemma of the international system. With and among states not much linked by these ties, the threat of violence remains.

Kant argued that the three elements of his pacific federation would strengthen over time to produce a more peaceful world. Individuals desire to be free and prosperous, so democracy and trade will expand, which leads naturally to the growth of international law and organization to facilitate these processes. Among Kantian republics, peace does not depend upon a moral transformation of humanity so long as even devils understand how to promote their own interests.[3] For Kant, a child of the Enlightenment, this was evidence of an ordered universe and, perhaps, of providential design. Yet it was not mechanical, nor did it provide a determined outcome. Reason would not always prevail; states and individuals would not always act as their enlightened interest might suggest. Human agents would have to learn from their own and others' experience, including the experience of war. A more peaceful world can be built, but human intelligence and volition are required to bring it about.

2. The Epidemiology of International Conflict

My purpose here is to offer evidence that the Kantian tradition is alive and well, not just as a prescription but also as a reasonably faithful description of much of contemporary international politics. Kant was not a wishful thinker. Though he lived in a time and place (Königsberg in 1795) which was no republic, and international law was weak, he did know something of actual republics, and his city was a trading state of the Hanseatic League. While he took his theory far beyond his experience, it was to some degree empirically informed. What astonishes me is how accurately it fits much of what we can now discern more systematically about how nations behave toward one another.

In this discussion I will draw on a body of analysis that I have carried out with several collaborators, especially John Oneal. I omit most of the customary technical discussion and scholarly references, but some relatively accessible presentations are available to the interested reader. Science, whether biological, physical, or social, is in part an adversary process, and scientific findings are always subject to development, modification, or refutation. Not everything I say is in the category of consensual knowledge; major parts are in some dispute. Nonetheless, much of the material I present is widely accepted, at least in broad outline, among social scientists of international relations.[4] I do not hope to persuade you that my subsequent statements are true, but only that they are plausible and worth serious attention.

To understand some of the influences that promote or inhibit war and conflict, I pursue an analogy between the way medical scientists seek to understand the causes of disease and the way social scientists now are seeking to understand the causes of conflict. In this section I discuss a basic approach characteristic of much medical research on the causes of disease, and then in the next provide a conceptual framework for analogous research on international conflict. After that, I explain how the epidemiological model and the conceptual framework can be combined in actual research to evaluate the realist and Kantian perspectives on international relations. In the conclusion I offer some brief comments on the relation of this research to Catholic traditions, and to the intersections of faith and science identified by some other contributors to this book.

3. An "Epidemiological" Method

The primary method we use falls under the label "the epidemiology of war and peace." National governments, and people who support them and die for them, sometimes willingly wage war or otherwise wield military force and the threat of large-scale physical violence. Nevertheless, most of the time most countries are at peace. A few, like Switzerland, have not engaged in a major military confrontation for a century or more. Many others have experienced war or a severe military-diplomatic crisis within the memory of their older citizens, but for the vast majority of the time their countries have been at peace. The usual condition, therefore, is peace, or at least the limited kind of peace implied by the absence of war. People typically desire peace not just for the absence of killing, but for the chance to live "normal" and perhaps prosperous lives. We expect our governments to preserve peace, consistent with maintaining national security.

For most individuals, their usual condition is a kind of health, or at least the absence of life-threatening disease. Although some fortunate and wisely-governed nations may avoid war indefinitely, individual human beings ultimately die. Still, most of us try to delay that day by all reasonable means, and the practitioners of medical science assist us. Medical researchers try, by a combination of theory and empirical research, to identify the conditions which promote or prevent fatal diseases.

Much of medical research is experimental or clinical and attendant to the details of particular cases, but a large proportion of it is "epidemiological" in character. That is, researchers are interested in the distribution of particular diseases in large populations, and the reasons why some individuals contract a disease and many others do not. Very large computerized data bases—about who dies where and when of various diseases, and about characteristics of the life experience and genetic heritage of those individuals—help the researchers to uncover the causes, and ultimately to devise regimes for prevention or treatment. Frequently these data bases include records on hundreds of thousands of individuals. These records are never fully accurate and complete, but if they are reasonably so, a skilled researcher with keen intuition or a sharply-honed theoretical hypothesis can perform statistical analyses on them to discover some of the conditions that are at least correlated with disease.

If the theory is sound and well-articulated, the researcher may well be able to move beyond simple correlations to suggest the causal mechanisms whereby something in individuals' heredity or environment actually produces the disease. This kind of epidemiological or "macro" research is rarely conclusive in establishing a causal mechanism, which typically must be confirmed by controlled experiments and micro-level studies of individual patients or the changes within their cells. Nonetheless, good macro-level epidemiological work can suggest where to look for plausible causal mechanisms and, even before the micro-level mechanisms are well understood, can provide very practical advice about what kinds of exposures or behaviors individuals should avoid if they wish to stay healthy. Such practical experience, in turn, together with medical theory, can help to inform the macro-researchers about what they might look for next. Reports of this kind of work appear almost daily in the newspapers.

Consider, for example, the kind of results which one would see in a large-scale "epidemiological" examination of the apparent causes of death from heart disease. Certain characteristics of individuals would readily emerge as strongly associated, perhaps causally, with the probability that any individual will die from heart disease. One obvious result of such a study would be that the chances that a person will die of heart disease increase as he or she ages. A second would be that the person's chances of a heart attack are greater if one or both parents died of heart disease—heredity. The researcher might not be able to tell just why a parent's heart disease increases the likelihood that a child will also experience it, but the empirical correlation would be apparent. Also, we know that on average males are more likely to die of heart attacks than are females when such other influences as age and heredity are held constant in the analysis. This first list is composed of influences over which the individual and medical advisers have little control. One cannot keep the years from advancing, cannot change one's parents, and—except at high and usually undesirable costs of various kinds—cannot change sex. So far, an advising physician can do little more than advise those patients seemingly at high risk to be sure they keep their life insurance paid up. And for some patients that could be valuable—if unwelcome—advice.

But of course neither patient nor physician will stop there, and other elements of the epidemiological research can be helpful in prevention. We now know that certain lifestyles or habits are associated with the risk of heart disease, and that these habits can, in principle, be modified. For instance, smokers run a much higher risk of heart attack than do non-smokers. So too do those who consume a diet high in cholesterol and saturated fats, or those who engage in little physical exercise. Each of these influences operates substantially independently of the others. That is, smoking by itself increases the risk of a heart attack whether or not one has a family history of heart disease and regardless of dietary intake. Therefore an advising physician can say something like the following: "Based on your age, sex, family history, and your lifestyle, statistically you run a 2 percent risk of having a heart attack in the next year. You can't totally eliminate that risk, but if you will quit smoking (or go on a diet, or get off the couch), you can cut that risk in half. In fact, if you will change your lifestyle fairly drastically—quit smoking, go on a diet, *and* get off the couch—you can cut your risk by three-quarters." In other words, "Some things are beyond your ability or mine to change or control, but a lot of other things can be done to improve your health if you want to do them badly enough."

None of these influences is a perfect predictor. Many people who do not smoke, or who give it up, nevertheless have heart attacks. Many smokers live a long time without a heart attack, ultimately dying of something else. The predictions are probabilistic, about greater and lesser risks, not about certainties. Moreover, the research that forms the basis for this advice is never perfect; estimates of the relative contribution of the different influences may change somewhat on the basis of subsequent research or better data: for example, data based on actually monitoring what people eat or how much they exercise, rather than what they tell a questioner about their eating and exercising habits. Further research on diet may establish particular kinds of foods or chemicals that make a special difference. And it will be impossible ever to get a perfect model to predict or explain all heart attacks, with no unexplained results. For such a complex biological phenomenon the theory can never be complete enough or precise enough. But at some point the medical community, or individual physicians and patients, decide the advice is reliable enough to act upon.

4. An Information Base on War and Conflict

It is now possible to do similar analyses on vital matters of war and peace. Although most people are reasonably healthy much of the time, the possiblity of serious disease or death is always inherent in the human condition. So too, though most countries are at peace most of the time, the possibility of serious military confrontation or war is always inherent in international relations. As with the medical studies, large-scale statistical analyses do not avoid the need to closely examine the experience of particular individuals or countries. Far from it. But the two very different methods can nicely complement each other, and it is the epidemiological analogy that I follow here.

Our data base, analogous to the life histories of individuals used by medical epidemiologists, consists of information on relations between virtually all countries in the world in each year over the period from 1885 to 1992. Full information on the years before and after does not yet exist. Still, we can cover the expansion and deepening of democracy, economic interdependence, and international organizations over a substantial span of time and examine their effects in different historical periods. Different historical periods may experience different configurations of power in international relations. Realists, for example, contrast multipolar with bipolar systems, usually defined by the number of major powers in the system. By this criterion, the international system was multipolar for centuries preceding 1945, but bipolar during the cold war. The post–World War II era, in its entirety, of course corresponds to the nuclear era. Many realists argue that the deterrent value of nuclear weapons also markedly changed the calculus of peace and war from that previously operating. The cold war ended sometime between 1988 and 1992, depending on how one judges the importance of different events. So we can hope to see the effect of greatly diminished bipolarity in the most recent data.

Since our basic perspective is that countries can in principle fight any other country, but in most instances are constrained from fighting particular countries, our information base is organized by pairs of countries, or *dyads*. For example, we are concerned not with Germany in general, but individually with relations between Germany and Austria, Belgium, France, Japan, Sweden, and so forth. This gives us over 150,000 "cases," where a case is the experience of *each pair of countries in each year*. From it we can compute the likelihood that a pair of countries sharing a certain constraint on conflict (for example, distance, a common alliance, or democratic forms of government) experienced a serious militarized dispute in any particular year, and how much lower their risk of conflict was than for the "average" pair of countries not experiencing that constraint.

We use information compiled by many scholars and organizations to carry out this analysis. For the more subjective information in particular, we rely on standardized sources that were in no way informed by our own judgments or biases about individual cases. For conflict we use data on militarized interstate disputes (MIDs). We are interested in all international militarized disputes, not just wars. Wars are rather rare events and, as with rare diseases, it is hard to find general patterns in where and why they erupt. Casting our net more widely, to include all organized uses of violence between countries, or threats to use violence, gives us a better chance to discern those general patterns. MIDs short of war are about twenty times as common as are wars. Also, hardly any wars erupt without some previous threat or more limited use of violence. Many militarized disputes have the potential to escalate to war if national leaders are not careful, and, where the evidence is plentiful enough, the influences and constraints on wars do not differ much from those on disputes in general. So it makes good sense to investigate the more inclusive phenomenon. We have a record of each year a dyad was involved in a dispute in which one or both governments threatened to use force, made a demonstration of force, or actually used military force against the other.

We look at a variety of influences on the emergence of disputes. Here I keep to a minimum the technical discussion of the sources, definitions, and decisions necessary to turn concepts and hypotheses into measures we can employ in systematic study. Readers who wish to examine these matters can do so in the materials listed in note four. The same is true for technical details about the statistical analysis, which proved highly complex. To minimize the likelihood that the supposed influences were themselves affected by the dispute to be explained (for instance, conflict can reduce trade as well as trade reduce conflict), we use the condition of all of them for the year prior to the year for which the existence of dispute or peace is recorded.

The inherent possibility of war means that states must find the policies, and the means, to look out for themselves. By force of arms, or the assistance of allies, or even by appeasement, they may seek to prevent the inherent possibility of international violence from becoming manifest. Some constraints on the use of violence exist already, and others can be created or enhanced. These constraints and the empirical measures of them we employed are of two kinds, realist and Kantian.

5. Realist Constraints

Distance. One constraint on the use of violence is simply physical distance and topography. Distance is the simplest: the farther away my potential enemy is, the less likely we are to fight (all other influences being equal, as in our discussion of the patient who gives up smoking). First of all, we will have less opportunity to fight. Most countries find it hard to exert great military power at a substantial distance. It is one thing to be able to mount an incursion across the border of an immediate neighbor, and quite another to invade a country thousands of miles away across water or the territory of other countries. The ability to use military power declines with distance. Secondly, states are less likely to have reasons to fight peoples in distant lands. The great majority of international wars and threats to go to war arise over territorial issues, chiefly the location of borders, the seizure or recovery of territory from a neighbor, or the ownership of valuable natural resources (oil, minerals, fishing grounds). Many conflicts arise over the treatment of ethnic minorities, such as groups of people who may be a majority in one country but an allegedly ill-treated minority in the other. The boundaries may have been delineated in a way that divides peoples who may identify with ethnically similar peoples across the border. Wherever borders are recent and ethnically artificial—as in contemporary Africa—the possibility that one country will intervene in another on behalf of an ethnic minority can be strong, an excuse if not necessarily a reason for war.

To account for the degree to which proximity raises the risk of a military dispute, two different measures are useful. One is the great circle distance on the surface of the earth between the two states' capitals. This is a reasonable measure of distance between home countries. But, as we move back in time, colonial holdings become geopolitically more important. Countries may have reason and ability to fight each other across colonial boundaries as well as home country to home country. Many international disputes, and some wars, began that way. We consider states contiguous if they or their colonies either share a land boundary or are separated by less than 150 miles of water.

Power. If proximity makes conflict and war likely, then distance is a constraint. But the constraint is much greater for small or weak countries (most of those in the world) than on those few countries we call great powers. A great power has the ability to exercise military force even at great distance. The cost to do so at a distance is greater than against a neighbor, but a great power typically has the resources to do it. Napoleon had the resources to move a huge army across Europe to invade Russia (though extending his lines of supply ultimately cost him dearly). In the eighteenth and nineteenth centuries great navies provided Britain with a capacity to build an empire, protected by the threat to use force, all around the globe. In the twentieth century, air power and eventually missiles with nuclear weapons provided the instruments whereby a state big and rich enough to afford them could strike anywhere. So, even though great powers too are constrained partly by distance, they alone have the ability on a regular basis to mitigate the effects of that constraint. And by acquiring colonies—or spheres of influence, or naval bases, or markets or sources of vital imports great distances away—they too are more likely to have reasons and a willingness to fight adversaries despite the distance.

Analysts commonly consider Britain, France, and Russia/the former Soviet Union to be major powers. Austria-Hungary is included until its defeat and dismemberment in 1918. Italy and Germany are included until their defeat in World War II, when both ceased to play a significant military role beyond their own borders. Japan, which became something of a great power after defeating China in 1895, also is excluded as a military actor after its defeat in 1945. The United States is included after its victory over Spain in 1898, and China after the communist takeover in 1949.

So we now have two types of dyads with the potential for conflict: contiguous states, and noncontiguous dyads containing at least one major military power. Together, they constitute what are called "politically relevant dyads," about 40,000 of them. Empirically they are twenty-four times more likely to experience a militarized dispute than are "irrelevant" ones. Overwhelmingly, then, these are the dyads at risk, and they are the ones for which I report the analyses below. Reducing the data base this way allows me to take the effect of distance, contiguity, and power status into account. Analyses of the full set of 150,000 dyads show similar effects for the different influences, save, of course, that the average risk is very much lower.

Power Ratio. One obvious way to constrain the likelihood of going to war is to deter it by military strength. Deterrence has long been a key element of statecraft. I will try to make myself strong enough to deter you from attacking me. I will be strong enough to deny you the ability to invade me successfully, except perhaps at a cost that will be far too high for you. Topography (mountains for Switzerland, the Atlantic and Pacific Oceans for the United States) can help in this strategy, but military strength will also matter, usually greatly. Or, if I cannot deny you the ability to invade me, I can punish you severely. This is fundamentally the strategy of nuclear deterrence: I cannot prevent the attack, but I can make you very sorry indeed.

Simply to focus on military strength, however, evades a key question. Does deterrence more often succeed simply by matching the other state's power, in effect by deterring both sides more or less equally? This is the basis for the school of thought that sees international peace as maintained by a balance of power. A balance may inhibit conflict because both states will be uncertain whether they can win a military conflict, and thus will be reluctant to start one. But maybe violent conflict is better constrained by a great predominance of power for one side. In the latter variation the weak state is deterred from provoking or attacking the strong one, but the reverse is not true. Some analysts contend that militarized disputes are in fact tests of national power under parity, and arise when both sides have very different expectations about which one will win. When power is very imbalanced the outcome of a possible violent conflict is usually predictable, and the much weaker side generally will not fight when it knows it will lose. In the words of Thucydides' history of the Peloponnesian wars, "the strong do as they will and the weak do as they must." Power predominance would constrain the resort to violence, but at the risk of dominance and exploitation. Relative power is a key variable in realists' thinking about the cause and prevention of war in international politics. I find the predominance hypothesis intuitively more plausible, but we investigate whether the empirical evidence better supports expectations of the balancers or the predominators.

We include a measure of the balance of power to see whether balanced or preponderant power is more likely to constrain conflict, and by how much. A standard composite measure of national power includes iron and steel production, population, military manpower, and military expenditures. Together, these tap a combination of elements that can be used immediately for military purposes (manpower and expenditures) and longer-term military potential relevant in a protracted conflict. No measure of power is perfect, especially over a century-long period that witnessed major innovations in technology and strategy, but this one is reasonable. Power ratio is the stronger state's capability index divided by that of the weaker member.

Allies. Another way to constrain military conflict is to form an alliance with another state. A major motive in forming an alliance is protection. Small states may seek an alliance with much bigger protectors. Or, preferring to avoid too close a relationship with a great power, they may seek to put together an alliance with one or more other small states. Big powers too may see security in alliances, either with another big power or with several small and strategically located states. Sometimes a big power may use an alliance as a means to control a smaller state and perhaps to keep it from acting provocatively with a regional adversary in a way that drags the big state unwillingly into a war. Allies do not usually fight or threaten each other with military action. They share important strategic and security interests. If they have military disputes among themselves, they risk weakening their common front against a country each perceives as an enemy. During the cold war, NATO allies (save for Greece and Turkey) did not dispute with each other to the point of inflicting casualties. Military conflicts among the Warsaw Pact countries were rare, but not unknown. Several times the Soviet Union intervened (in Hungary in 1956, Czechoslovakia in 1968) or threatened its smaller allies to keep them from changing their governments and possibly leaving the alliance. Being allied certainly provides no guarantee that countries will avoid military conflict. We need to find out how important a mutual alliance really is in reducing the risk of a militarized dispute. We do that here, identifying the dyad by a numerical code of +1 if the two states were allied in a mutual defense treaty, a neutrality pact, or an entente, and by 0 otherwise.

Distance, and to a large degree the ability to be a great power, are not matters over which most states have much control. They are more like givens, more like individuals' age, family history, and sex in our health example. Relative power—particularly the degree to which a state chooses to devote resources to building up its relative military power—and alliances, however, are much more like diet and exercise, over which an individual can often exercise a good deal of control. Yet all share the common characteristic of being familiar elements of realist theories, and are also understood by Kant as constraints on the use of violence.

6. Kantian Constraints

Kantians (liberal institutionalists), however, insist that the realist perspective alone is incomplete. Especially, the realists do not exhaust the list of constraints on war over which states can and do exercise some control. A positive peace would rest on the three Kantian supports as well as on power politics. States do not fight all others at all times and places where the realist constraints are weak. To the realist influences we add the three Kantian influences, hypothesizing that democracies will be constrained from using force, especially against other democracies; that economically important trade creates incentives for the maintenance of peaceful relations; and that international organizations constrain decision makers by positively promoting peace in a variety of ways. Since the modern international system is far from being a "pacific federation" of democratic states, we expect both realist and Kantian factors to affect interstate relations.

Democracy. The first of the Kantian influences produces the expectation that democracies will rarely fight or even threaten each other, and perhaps the additional expectation that democracies will be more peaceful in general, with all kinds of states. Many studies by now have produced support for the first proposition (democracies rarely fight each other); the assertion that democracies are more peaceful in general is more controversial, but is becoming more widely accepted. Theoretical explanations of why democracies are more peaceful, especially toward one another, are less consensual. Plausible explanations, in simple form, include the following.

Normatively, democracies operate internally on the principle that conflicts are to be resolved peacefully by negotiation and compromise, without resort to the threat or use of organized violence. Democratic peoples and their leaders recognize other democracies as operating under the same principles in their internal relations, and so extend to them the principle of peaceful conflict resolution internationally. Thus negotiation and compromise between democratic states are expected, and the threat of violence is illegitimate as well as probably unnecessary. Authoritarian states, by contrast, are expected to operate more on Hobbesian principles, making threats, taking advantage of weakness of resolve, and using force. Thus in their relations with authoritarian states democracies will not experience the same restraints.

Democratic leaders who fight a war are held responsible, through democratic institutions, for the costs and benefits of the war. The costs often outweigh the benefits, and many of the costs are borne by the general public. Democratic leaders who fight wars—especially if they lose, and often even if they don't—are likely to be voted out of office. There is good evidence for this. In anticipating this political judgment, democratic leaders will be reluctant to fight wars, especially wars they are likely to lose. When facing another democracy, both sets of leaders will be restrained. Authoritarian leaders, however, are better able to repress opposition and to stay in power after a war. Moreover, by repression they can keep more of the benefits and impose more of the costs on their peoples than can democratic leaders. So they will be less hesitant to fight.

Democratic government is relatively transparent. When the country is united in a policy toward another state, the leaders can bargain and threaten more credibly, thanks to this united resolve. But if the country is not united, the leaders' international credibility is undercut, and they will be more cautious about making threats that the country would not support. The opacity of authoritarian politics, however, becomes a disadvantage. Democracies are thus more credible bargainers when they threaten, and less likely to stumble into wars they really did not want to fight.

There is significant empirical support for each of the above variants. My best guess is that they all operate most of the time, with one more powerful than another in different circumstances. It is important to notice, however, that whereas the first represents a kind of normative restraint about right behavior, the second and third are straightforward rationalist explanations: peace can be maintained by leaders who pursue their own self-interest in domestic and international relations combined, regardless of normative influences. Kant's understanding of devils who, by institutional constraints, can be made to behave like angels, captures these perspectives.

The measure of democracy we used (compiled by others) is based on the presence of several restraints on government: (1) the presence of institutions and procedures through which most citizens can vote for alternative political policies and leaders; (2) the existence of institutionalized constraints on the exercise of executive power; and (3) the guarantee of rights to all citizens in their political expression and participation. These are the commonly specified criteria for democratic government. They do not accept as "democratic" every state that contains the name democracy in its official title; they overtly exclude the "people's republics" (or, occasionally, the "people's democratic republics") of communist states. The underlying idea is that the institutions, principles, and practices of democracy as it evolved first in the West—but now operative in countries all over the globe—provide powerful constraints on arbitrary government, constraints that are usually much weaker in political systems that lack those institutions and practices.

No democracy is perfect, nor are even the most totalitarian governments totally without restraints on arbitrary rule. Many states combine some mixture of democratic and authoritarian features. Democracy must be understood as a continuous measure, like exercise, or cholesterol level, or blood pressure. So each country is coded on a scale of +10 to -10 to test the hypothesis that the higher the degree of democracy the greater the constraint on its leadership in engaging in militarized disputes with other countries. A dispute can result from the actions of either state. Nonetheless, it is more plausible that the likelihood of conflict is primarily a result of the degree of constraint experienced by the less constrained state in each dyad. In effect, that state is the weak link in the chain of peaceful relations. We expect, therefore, that the less democratic state in a dyad most strongly raises the risk of interstate violence: the more democratic that state, the more constrained from engaging in a dispute it is likely to be.

International trade. Commercial interaction has a solid place among other parents of the liberal tradition, as well as Kant. By some views, broad and sustained commercial interaction becomes a medium of communication, a means whereby information about needs and preferences are exchanged, across a broad range of matters extending well beyond the specific commercial exchange. This may result in greater mutual understanding, empathy, and mutual identity across boundaries.

Another view (both complementary and alternative) stresses the self-interests of rational actors. Trade depends on expectations of peace with the trading partner. Violent conflict threatens one's access to markets, imports, and capital. Wars and militarized disputes, if they do not make trade between disputing states impossible, certainly raise the risks and costs. Hence, with our usual *ceteris paribus* assumption, the larger the share of trade between two countries contributes to the national economy of each, the stronger the potential political base with a material interest in preserving peaceful relations between them. This perspective contradicts other arguments that sentiments of exploitation may stimulate conflict between economically dependent units.

We measure the importance of trade for each state as the sum of its imports from and exports to the other, in each case divided by the state's gross national product. Trade data are from the International Monetary Fund, and GDP estimates are the best internationally accepted standard. Note that a given volume of trade will impact a small country much more than a big one. So, as with the effect of democracy, we employ the weak link assumption that conflict is inhibited least in the state less impacted by joint trade, and measure interdependence for the less trade-dependent state. (Surprisingly, we have found that asymmetric trade dependence does not in itself raise the probability of military conflict.) It would be good to have a similar measure for the effect of international investment, but the necessary data do not exist.

International organizations. Intergovernmental organizations (IGOs) are relatively recent phenomena in international politics. The first still-extant IGOs date from the nineteenth century, and most were formed after 1945. They include both quasi-universal organizations (like the UN or the IMF) and organizations focused on particular types of countries or regions. They may be either multi-purpose, or else "functional" agencies directed particularly to military security, promoting international commerce and investment, health, environmental concerns, marketing, human rights, or other purposes. The means by which they may promote peace also vary greatly, on a range that for some organizations may include coercing norm-breakers, mediating among conflicting parties, reducing uncertainty by providing information, expanding members' material interests to be more inclusive and longer-term, shaping norms, and generating narratives of mutual identification. International organizations vary widely by the means they employ and the effectiveness with which they do so. Again, one can discern elements of building normative restraints by changing perceptions and behavior, and elements of bringing the influence of self-interest into line with a collective interest—of making governments and their citizens think a bit more like angels, and of making even devilish ones behave better if they wish to survive and prosper.

The network of international organizations is spread very unevenly across the globe. Some dyads in Europe share membership in roughly 130 IGOs; other dyads share few or even none (e.g., the United States and the People's Republic of China during much of the cold war). Our measure here is the number of IGOs to which both members of the dyad belong. This is a crude index, equating all types and strengths of IGOs in a simple count. In principle one could develop a more refined measure, taking into account different organizational functions and purposes, but that is not possible yet. Using such a simple measure means that, if anything, we are likely to underestimate the conflict-reducing effect of IGOs. It would also be good in principle to look for the effect of international nongovernmental organizations (INGOs), but that too is not yet possible.

7. Analyzing the Global Experience of a Century

To uncover the relative importance of each of these influences on the likelihood of international conflict—the risk that dyads will engage in militarized disputes—we use a statistical method like that employed by epidemiologists to study the influences of environment, heredity, and life experience on illness. It is similar to what statisticians call multiple regression analysis; it estimates the independent effect of each of these variables while holding the effect of all the other variables constant. With the heart disease example, it tells how much the average patient's risk of a heart attack would be reduced if her blood cholesterol level were twenty points lower, or if she were not a smoker. By "independent effect" we mean the effect of changes in just one variable alone. With militarized disputes, we ask how much lower the risk would be if the two countries were allied, or if they were both democratic.

The table presents the percentage change in the risk to a contiguous dyad associated with a change in each variable plausibly subject to policy intervention.[5] The percentages are computed for a given amount of change in each successive coefficient while holding all the other coefficients constant at their baseline values—usually the average. The unit of change in the estimated coefficient, its standard deviation from the average, is measured relative to the total range of the variable. In the famous "bell curve" of a normal distribution, about 68 percent of all the observations fall within one standard deviation. By using this unit we make the different measures comparable so as to have a common unit for assessing the relative impact of each variable. (The exception is the binary variable for alliance, where the full range must be used, exaggerating its impact relative to the other influences where the change covers only a part of the range, the standard deviation.) The percentages should not be interpreted as precise, but as reasonable approximations from a still new and evolving research enterprise. Remember also that these are for politically relevant dyads, where contiguity and/or major power status have already made them much more dispute-prone than are all dyads. On average, the chances of a dispute in any year are a little over 5 percent, meaning that even these dyads avoid it most of the time.

Percentage Risk Change for Annual Involvement in a Militarized Dispute, Politically Relevant Pairs of States, 1886–1992

All influences at average values except:	
ALLIES equals 1	−40%
POWER RATIO increased by 1 standard deviation	−36%
LOWER DEMOCRACY increased by 1 standard deviation	−33%
LOWER DEMOCRACY decreased by 1 standard deviation	+48%
LOWER INTERDEPENDENCY increased by 1 standard deviation	−43%
IGO increased by 1 standard deviation	−24%

LOWER DEMOCRACY, LOWER INTERDEPENDENCY, and IGO all increased by 1 standard deviation

Some of the regularities are what realist theorists predict; for example, conflicts between allies are 40 percent less likely than between unallied states. Also, the predominance version of power theories is quite strongly supported; disproportionate power often deters weak states from challenging or resisting strong ones. If the relative power of the stronger state were increased by a standard unit, the chances of a militarized dispute emerging would be reduced by 36 percent.

Kantian theories, which recognize the exigencies of power politics, are consistent with these results. Yet we also find relationships that realist theory does not predict but a Kantian perspective does. For example, if the less democratic state were a standard unit more democratic than average, the frequency (predicted probability) of conflict would be 33 percent lower. Conversely, if the less democratic country were even less democratic by a standard unit, the likelihood of conflict would go up by 48 percent. Further scrutiny finds that militarized disputes between strongly democratic states are quite rare, and disputes between very authoritarian states are moderately common. Conflicts are most likely in dyads where one state is very democratic and the other is very authoritarian. These potentially hostile "cats and dogs" of world politics don't always fight, but often do. Economic interdependence has about the same effect as does democracy. If the less dependent state were a standard unit more dependent on trade with the other, the chance of a dispute would go down by 43 percent. The effect of IGOs is weakest, but even there the impact of a standard unit increase is to cut the risk of a militarized dispute by nearly one quarter. If all three Kantian variables—democracy, trade, and IGOs   are increased together, the risk of conflict drops by more than 70 percent.

These patterns largely apply throughout most of the more than one hundred years (1885–1992) covered by the study. They are not just phenomena of the bipolar nuclear era, of cold war security concerns, or of the unity of democratic capitalists against communists. When we break the evidence up into some smaller periods, much the same relationships apply. Essentially the same patterns exist for the pre–cold war era.[6] And, while information on the post–cold war years is limited to four years and so gives only early results, democracy, economic interdependence, and IGOs make significant contributions then, too.

This essential stability suggests another perspective from which to examine this information—that of the international system. Changes over time in the average level of democracy, interdependence, and IGO involvement capture not just dyadic phenomena but elements of the norms and institutions of the international system. Perhaps the world is no longer quite as Hobbesian as it was in previous eras. It was once common for wars and aggression simply to eliminate states. But whereas twenty-two internationally-recognized states were forcibly occupied or absorbed during the first half of the twentieth century, no state has lost its sovereignty through conquest since World War II. The emergence of a Kantian subsystem of states within which the use of force is illegitimate—indicated by the results presented above—might bring some further change at the global level, to the degree that the norms and institutions of this Kantian subsystem reduced the probability that force will be used even by states that are not democratic, interdependent, or bound by IGOs.

If democracies are more likely to win their wars than are autocracies, as the proportion of democracies in the international system grows, autocracies must be more concerned about the security implications of weakening themselves in war, either with democracies or with other autocracies. If most great powers become democratic, peace among them would reduce the incentive for wars involving nondemocratic states across great power spheres of influence. If liberalization spreads and stimulates economic growth among interdependent states, nonliberal states will have to be concerned lest they be punished by global markets for being the instigators of international violence that disrupts trade and investment; even antagonistic dyads with little mutual trade may find it prudent to abstain from violence. If international norms and institutions for resolving disputes grow, even nonliberal states may be impelled to use regional or international organizations to help settle their disputes rather than to accept the political, military, and economic costs from the liberal community that would increasingly result from the use of military force. Thus increases in the Kantian influences at the system level may beneficially affect the behavior even of dyads that are not democratic, dependent upon their bilateral trade, or involved in international organizations.

8. Some Conclusions about this Order in Anarchy

Compared with the typical pair of states, democracies rarely fight one another, economically interdependent countries rarely fight one another, and a dense network of international organizations often can inhibit violence. Some countries, though not all, learn to live peaceably with each other despite a centuries-long history of desperate, violent competition.

They may still have sharp economic and political disputes, but those disputes rarely become militarized, risking the use of force. The European Union—created deliberately by leaders and citizens—testifies to this possibility. None of this constitutes a deterministic law of behavior, but each represents the same kind of probability statement that a medical researcher can make about the risk that a smoker runs of developing lung cancer, relative to that of a nonsmoker. And like the medical research, it suggests points of intervention, like giving up smoking. Countries can support the emergence of democratic government in other countries, build economic ties with them, and construct cross-national organizations.

Moreover, Kant's vision was not of a simple set of independent influences on peace. Rather, he is better understood as describing a dynamic system of influences, in what we would now call feedback loops. Democratic states, preferring trading partners where property rights are secured by a rule of law, tend to trade more with each other than with autocracies. Democracies and trading partners are more likely to form or join international organizations. Thus the various elements of Kant's three supports to a structure of peace also support each other in producing his peaceful "federation" of commercial republics under international law. And in turn, peace encourages trade and facilitates the establishment of international organizations. Each of these relationships finds empirical support.[7]

In all this I see systematic evidence that cooperative international relations, which greatly reduce the probability of war, are possible and indeed are far more common than many people recognize. When one looks carefully for it, there is an order to be discerned and nurtured within the anarchy. It is the assumption that everyone is a potential enemy, not anarchy itself, that drives the Hobbesian security dilemma. Yet not all kinds of nations rage together. Many can and do get along in a condition of peace with many others, only rarely threatening to use military force against one another, let alone actually using it. They operate substantially by principles of negotiation and compromise, in an order of cooperation and reciprocation broadly consistent with basic precepts of moral behavior. This kind of order does not demand a moral transformation of humanity so much as it requires a careful structuring of relationships to channel self-interest in directions of mutual benefit. Within this order a norm of nonviolence can and should operate.

This order, however, does not apply equally to all states. Those not linked by common ties of democracy, economic interdependence, and international institutions have a much weaker basis for cooperation. That is especially true for pairs where both states lie largely outside this order vis-à-vis all others (e.g., Iran and Iraq). For these states, considerations of power and deterrence dominate many or most of their relationships. And it applies poorly to those pairs of states where one state may be enmeshed in many Kantian relationships of order, but the other either is largely devoid of such relationships or is engaged in another non-overlapping set (e.g., Israel vs. its Arab neighbors). For most of the economically developed democracies this is the condition in which they now exist. They are in stable peaceful relationships with one another, but have yet to find the means to overcome the anarchy of their relations with Libya, or North Korea, or Iraq. Still, they may strive to create more stable relationships, often stumblingly, as with China. In those cases the Kantian linkages are still weak, and the Hobbesian dilemma is always present.

Despite Kant's great philosophical differences with Catholicism, the elements of his understanding of international relations are not alien to the Catholic tradition, recent or ancient. With Kant, Catholic traditions dispute the realist vision of absolute state sovereignty and urge that persons are born to community. Some of these communities lie within state boundaries, others transcend them. Catholicism embraced democracy only lately, but following Pope John XXIII's *Pacem in Terris* the link became strong in theory and practice. *Gaudium et Spes* (par. 75), deeply informed by John Courtney Murray's understanding of democratic pluralism, called for political structures providing to all citizens "the practical possibility of freely and actively taking part in the establishment of the juridical foundations of the political community and in the direction of public affairs . . . and in the election of political leaders."[8] Catholic endorsement of economic liberalism is more restrained. Yet in *Centesimus Annus* Pope John Paul II, while expressing serious reservations about the forces of capitalism, accepted (par. 34) that "on the level of individual nations and international relations the free market is the most efficient instrument for utilizing resources and effectively responding to needs." *Pacem in Terris* (par. 137–39) required an "international public authority" to establish the peace of political community on a global scale. It would respect the legitimate claims of national sovereignty but have as "its fundamental objective the recognition, respect, safeguarding, and promotion of the rights of the human person." Others would identify also the role of regional international organizations, under the principle of subsidiarity. Subsequent popes have differed with the United Nations on some issues, but their support for the organization has been unflagging. *Centesimus Annus* (and John Paul II's earlier *Solicitudo Rei Socialis*) endorsed not only familiar economic, political, and social rights embedded in the Universal Declaration of Human Rights, but (par. 27) a commitment to building international structures capable of arbitrating and intervening in conflicts between nations.[9]

Not all these statements make a direct connection between their desired instruments and international peace. There is no single unified Catholic view on the possibility of peace. Not all reasonable Catholics accept the strong version of John XXIII's emphasis on a global authority, or are enthusiastic about the unalloyed merits of free trade. All good things do not necessarily go together. There is no free lunch. Democratic liberties can be debased, the inequalities of capitalism may run wild, a global authority could become a leviathan, peace does not always mean justice. But in this world, the roots of peace lie not simply in force, but in structured freedoms, and this may well be the best package for which to strive.

Finally, the evidence for an alternative and partially realized conception of international relations speaks to me of a created order—a sinful order, to be sure—that leaves us an opening for behavior that can be other-regarding while still self-regarding, imperfect, but not condemning us to a choice between self-victimization and endless cycles of violence. It is what John Polkinghorne calls, in his essay in this volume, a "rational created order," though one known only "in its cloudiness and probabilistic fitfulness." By a combination of Alan Wolfe's empirical truth and deduction, social science can help us to discern the music of the social spheres. It is part of "the integrated understanding of the order of things" toward which Alasdair MacIntyre urges us. "For the prayerful listener, the world becomes the sublime scripture, full of stories of structure and chaos, law and chance, complexification and decay."[10] I lack the capacity to work out the philosophical and theological implications of all this. But scholars do have the capacity, however flawed and incomplete, to discover these patterns and begin to understand them. They suggest the hand of a demanding but benevolent creator. Even when viewing a world of conflict, we can be moderate optimists and possibly better Christians.[11]

NOTES

I thank Claudio Cioffi-Revilla, J. Bryan Hehir, and Cynthia Russett for comments without burdening them with any responsibility.

1. I owe the term "modified realism" to Jean Bethke Elshtain, in her edited volume *Just War Theory* (New York: New York University Press, 1992). George Weigel, *Tranquilitas Ordinis* (New York: Oxford University Press, 1987), makes it the keystone of his "moderate realism" structure of the Augustinian tranquility of order. I have tried to interpret and strengthen the just war tradition, as in "Ethical Dilemmas of Nuclear Deterrence," *International Security* 8, 4 (Spring 1984): 36–54, and "Is NATO's War Just? Questions about Kosovo," *Commonweal,* 21 May 1999, 13–15.

2. Immanuel Kant, *Perpetual Peace: A Philosophical Sketch*, in *Kant's Political Writings*, ed. Hans Reiss (Cambridge: Cambridge University Press, 1970), 105; James Bohman and Matthias Lutz-Bachmann, eds., *Perpetual Peace: Essays on Kant's Cosmopolitan Ideal* (Cambridge, Mass.: M.I.T. Press, 1997).

3. Kant, *Perpetual Peace*, 112.

4. Research reports include Bruce Russett, *Grasping the Democratic Peace: Principles for a Post–Cold War World* (Princeton, N.J.: Princeton University Press, 1993); Russett, John R. Oneal, and David R. Davis, "The Third Leg of the Kantian Tripod: International Organizations and Militarized Disputes, 1950–85," *International Organization* 52 (1997): 267–94; Oneal and Russett, "The Kantian Peace: The Pacific Benefits of Democracy, Interdependence, and International Organizations, 1885–1992," *World Politics* 52 (1999). The findings I discuss here are from the last. A full report is Russett and Oneal, *Triangulating Peace: Democracy, Interdependence, and International Organizations* (New York: Norton, 2001).

5. The method—logistic regression analysis—differs from standard multiple regression analysis because the dependent variable is nominal (a dispute, or no dispute) rather than continuous (small dispute, big dispute, war). With the dyad-year as unit of analysis the data set combines the effect of dyads' differences over time and their differences within any year. This kind of analysis is mathematically complex, requiring adjustments because many observations are not truly independent. For instance, a German attack on Belgium was certain to bring France into war, and once Germany and France were at war it was more likely that they would still be at war in the following year. Methodologists still are working on some of these analytical problems. The analysis here employs standard statistical corrections to prevent us from exaggerating the effect of our variables. It is conventional to present regression coefficients and measures of the statistical significance of each, but it is easier to grasp the intuitive meaning of the risk reduction percentages. The coefficients underlying each of these percentages are all highly significant statistically; i.e., the odds that the sign of the coefficient should be the opposite from what I find are less than 2 in 1000.

6. For these periods, shorter than the cold war era and with a vastly smaller international system, more reliable patterns can be found only by including all dyads, not just the politically relevant ones. Even so, if one cuts up the long 1885–1939 period further, the basic relationships do vary, with the no effect of democracy before about 1900 or for interdependence between the World Wars. Only when one keeps the full period intact does its resemblance to the cold war era emerge clearly.

7. See my "A Neo-Kantian Perspective: Democracy, Interdependence, and International Organizations in Developing Security Communities," in Emanuel Adler and Michael Barnett, eds., *Security Communities* (New York: Cambridge University Press, 1998).

8. Of course, one must look more widely than just at statements of the magisterium to discern Catholic values. On the broad acceptance of democracy, see, for example, Erik Hansen, *The Catholic Church in World Politics* (Princeton, N.J.: Princeton University Press, 1987), and John Langan, "The Catholic Vision of World Affairs," *Orbis* 42 (1998): 241–61.

9. See Mary Ann Glendon's essay in this volume on Catholic input to the Universal Declaration, which included (art. 28) "a social and international order in which the rights and freedoms set forth in this Declaration can be fully realized."

10. Chet Raymo, "Heeding the New Creation Story," *Commonweal,* 5 June 1998, 13.

11. Perhaps conforming with the instruction from *Gaudium et Spes* (par. 62), "May the faithful . . . blend modern science and its theories and the understanding of the most recent discoveries with Christian morality and doctrine. Thus their religious practice and morality can keep pace with their scientific knowledge," and from *Fides et Ratio* (par. 19), "From the greatness and beauty of created things comes a corresponding perception of their creator." Possibly the role is to be one of the "vessels which history fashions in every period for men who must keep [the Word] in their own hearts and then hand it down in the words their own civilization has taught them" (Jean Leclercq, *The Love of Learning and the Desire for God*, 3d ed. [New York: Fordham University Press, 1982], 258).

5

"Art," Literature, Theology

Learning from Germany

NICHOLAS BOYLE

IN 1998 MY COLLEGE IN CAMBRIDGE CELEBRATED THE CENTENARY of the birth of one of its best-known fellows, the literary critic, religious apologist, and children's author, C. S. Lewis. I hoped that during the celebrations, which included extensive readings from Lewis's works and commentaries on them, I would at last track down the location of a remark of his which has always intrigued and impressed me. I hoped in vain. In a footnote, I think, to one of his numerous minor essays, Lewis, one of the most serious twentieth-century thinkers about the relation between Christianity and literature, remarks that "art and aesthetics" are terms that have meant little to him in his lifelong dealings with the great written monuments of European civilization; he has instead preferred to think of what he has been doing in terms of "literature and criticism." This double distinction between "art" and "literature," "aesthetics" and "criticism," is the fundamental distinction underlying what I have to say here. I believe that distinction has a certain theological significance, both in the sense that it derives from a certain episode in the history of theology, and in the sense that it is relevant to the question of how theology should be done today. Hence the first part of my title: "Art" as opposed to "literature"—this, I am saying, is a distinction with theological implications.

What about the second part of my title: "Learning from Germany"? It is, I am afraid, a pun. For on the one hand the modern university disciplines of theology, literary studies, at least in some areas, and the study of art—whether by that we mean more narrowly the history of the visual arts, or more broadly the philosophical discipline of aesthetics—have all been profoundly influenced by German developments, even when they are not simply wholesale importations of German learning. And on the other hand I think that there are certain lessons to be learned from the German example about how we should conduct ourselves in the modern academy, particularly in those areas where "art," literature, and theology are coming together and seeking to learn from one another. So both the first and the second halves of my title point to a contemporary lesson to be learned, even though much of what I have to say will be in the nature of historical musings. The lesson might be something like this: the integration, to use Professor MacIntyre's word, of literature and theology should not be difficult in principle, since modern literary studies, and modern literature itself, have to some extent a theological origin; in detail, however, the integration is likely to be problematic, particularly perhaps for an American Catholic university.

I shall first, and at some length, address the interrelation of "art," literature, and theology in the German context. Then, with a brevity proportionate to my ignorance of the subject, I shall make some suggestions about a possible American context in which to see these matters. Thirdly and finally, I shall address one particular area of contemporary Catholic interest.

If I begin by turning my attention to eighteenth-century Germany, that is not only because that is the subject I know most about. It is also because that is a subject which I think it is worth knowing about if you are interested in modern theology, philosophy, or the theory of art and literature, and particularly if you are interested in modern institutions of higher education, the subjects taught in them—especially in the humanities faculties—and their relationship to the society which they serve. It is well known that in the late eighteenth and early nineteenth centuries Germany experienced something like a second Renaissance, a flowering of literature, philosophy, and music without parallel elsewhere in contemporary Europe, though it soon came to be a crucial force inspiring and sustaining what we now see as the continental, or even intercontinental, movement of romanticism. What is less well appreciated is the essential role played in this cultural renaissance, and in its successor movements down to our own days, by the German universities.

The German university system is a phenomenon of unique and largely unstudied significance in the history of European and ultimately of world culture. It has provided an institutional continuity within German intellectual life through the upheavals of two centuries—German states and nations have come and gone but the German universities have carried on regardless, barring a couple of episodes of denazification and deleninization. There is nothing in non-German philosophy to set beside the extraordinarily continuous German tradition passing down by reaction and often parricidal renewal from one professorial generation to the next, from Wolff to Kant to Hegel to neo-Kantianism, phenomenology, Heidegger, and Habermas. Even those figures who might seem to stand outside it are related to it by the emotive or scandalous circumstances in which they rejected it or were expelled from it—Schopenhauer, Feuerbach, Marx, Nietzsche, Adorno. The system which provided the context and shelter for this uniquely sustained philosophical conversation of over 250 years' duration, and which was given its definitive form by Wilhelm von Humboldt during his time as a Prussian minister, was effectively given the status of a global standard in the later nineteenth century when it was adopted with enthusiasm in Japan and rather more reluctantly in the U.S.A., and when it served as the basis for a rather cautious reform of the British universities.

But even before Humboldt, who only simplified and rationalized what he found already in existence, the German universities made up a social and intellectual engine of awesome power. In the eighteenth century there were between forty and fifty of them, at a time when England could boast only two, and the not uncommon new foundations were a sign that the system was healthy and energetic—twenty-four in two centuries, some of which rapidly became leading universities of Europe, such as Halle (founded 1694) and Göttingen (founded 1737). Impressive though they were, however, as centers for the study of law, medicine, theology, and the cameral, or economic, sciences, and after the middle of the eighteenth century for the study also of more modern subjects such as the natural sciences, history, philological disciplines, and philosophy, the universities were not maintained out of a disinterested love of learning. They were inseparable from the social and political structure of the territories within which they were situated and which provided their funding. The faculties had only limited powers of self-government and were largely administered by nonacademic bureaucrats. The professors were state employees and took an oath of loyalty to the sovereign. Territorial rulers, notably the kings of Prussia, made repeated efforts to prevent their subjects from studying anywhere but at their own state universities. At Göttingen the purpose of the university was succinctly summarized as to produce "useful servants of the state, more precisely, servants of this territorial prince."[1] This is the nub of the matter: the German university system existed to educate state officials—civil servants: lawyers, most obviously, but also in the Protestant territories the crypto-officialdom of the clergy and of the schoolteachers (organized by the ecclesiastical consistory), all of whom were salaried by the state. Not merely did the professors educate civil servants (and clergymen), they themselves often had been, or were destined to become, administrative officials or, in the case of theologians, exercised hierarchical authority. And it was this class of more or less overt state officials that produced the German Renaissance of the late eighteenth century, the classical and romantic culture of the German nation-to-be. Social historians have called this group—the group which throughout the late eighteenth and the nineteenth century dominated both intellectual life and the political struggle for national unity—*die Gebildeten*: a word which may be translated as "the cultured classes," but which also means simply "the educated classes," those who have been to university.[2] "More than anything else," T. C. W. Blanning has written, "it was this academic-bureaucratic predominance which distinguished German culture in the eighteenth century."[3]

It is vitally important to realize that the middle class which made the German cultural revolution was not composed of traders, proprietors, or even independent professionals, like the class which made the American and French revolutions or founded the second British Empire. The strata of society in which the second German Renaissance of 1780–1815 was rooted were not the ossified *grands bourgeois* of the no doubt free but politically ever more insignificant free cities of the Holy Roman Empire, nor the economically successful but politically emasculated commercial bourgeoisie of the unfree cities Leipzig and Berlin. Rather they were the castes which, though distributed across the whole of Germany, everywhere stood in a direct relation to the local, monarchical state power: the Protestant clergy, the professorate, and the other subdivisions of state-salaried officialdom. At the beginning of the eighteenth century the German middle class was far too weak to follow the English or Dutch example and to seize back the power that the princes had wrested from the urban bourgeoisie after the catastrophe of the Thirty Years' War. But by means of a long march through the institutions, and in the guise of a class not of independent capitalists but of dependent officials, it succeeded in making an alliance with the nobility, above all the lower nobility. This "mixed stratum of noble and bourgeois origin"[4]—or as Hegel, one of its most illustrious representatives, called it, this "universal class"[5]—succeeded in gaining "a partial victory over monarchical absolutism"[6] and ushered in instead the age of absolutist bureaucracy.

Germany's cultural flowering in the last third of the eighteenth century can only be understood as part of this process. It was the work of an intelligentsia whose members were trained at universities intended to be "a career-ladder into the ranks of the clergy and the bureaucracy," and who saw their personal lives as success or failure in such a career, or as a variation on it.[7] The clergy were a particularly important group in this university-trained intelligentsia. In the class of *die Gebildeten* the clergy were the specific vehicle of cultural values: reflection about human beings, and their individual and collective purposes, about morality and psychology, was of the essence of their social task, even if they were not Pietists. In Protestant territories they performed that task as officers of the state: indeed in rural areas they might explicitly discharge the duties of a bailiff, superintending road repairs for example.[8] The state was closely interested in their education; theology was much the best endowed subject at all universities; and the availability of scholarships and the prospect of a secure position made it a natural course for a poor young man of ability to embark on a theological career as a way to advance himself. This, for example, was exactly the pattern of the early careers of Winckelmann and Fichte, who both came from desperately poor backgrounds, and the famous three students of the Tübingen seminary around 1790—Hölderlin, Hegel, and Schelling—were there as a result of a deliberate policy of educating bright boys from an early age for the ministry. The special importance of the clerical subdivision of *die Gebildeten* was appreciated over seventy years ago by Herbert Schöffler in his pioneering study *Protestantismus und Literatur*. He drew up a list of 120 German writers—from which, incidentally, philosophers are excluded—born between 1676 and 1804 who either studied theology or were the sons of theologians. (These include Gottsched, Gellert, Klopstock, Lessing, Hamann, Wieland, Matthias Claudius, Lichtenberg, Hölty, Herder, Bürger, Lenz, Klinger, K. P. Moritz, Jean Paul, the brothers Schlegel, Hölderlin, and Mörike.) And Schöffler's crucial point is that, despite their training or background, almost none of these founders of modern German literature—and, I believe we should add, philosophy—pursued a clerical vocation.[9]

The German literary renaissance has to be understood as the consequence of the secularization of the clerical class and its social function. In the course of the eighteenth century the German clergy drifted into intellectual and existential crisis—partly as a result of an over-production of theologians brought about by the state itself, partly as a result of a subversion of the authority of the Bible through new developments in philosophy and critical scholarship. The sons of pastors whose faith was insecure and whose prospects were unsatisfactory looked about for a new way of life and a new content for existence; students of theology changed to different subjects, in part the subjects newly introduced into the new philosophical faculties which began to be founded in the later part of the century. Schöffler thus summarizes his conclusions:

> Ministers take an ever-increasing interest in general literature; young students of theology attract and hold the attention of their contemporaries by works on the borderline between the older devotional literature and literature proper; the sons of the clergy, like many of their fellow-students, abandon the study of theology with increasing frequency as Enlightenment spreads, or when they have finished their studies do not enter the church. From 1740, at all events, clergy, their sons and young theologians generally, come into literature in shoals, so that from the middle of the century its total aspect undergoes a great change.[10]

Publishing statistics bear out Schöffler's generalization. In 1740, 19 percent of all German books published were popular works of theology intended for the layperson, while imaginative literature made up only 6 percent of the total. In 1800, however, the situation was exactly reversed: popular theology had shrunk to only 6 percent, while imaginative literature now ran to 21 percent.[11] What this new secular literature amounted to in its most refined form is well summarized for us by the great cultural historian of Germany, W. H. Bruford:

> Although the critical zeal of the Aufklärung in Germany, once it had got under way, stopped at nothing in its search for truth, a series of profound and learned thinkers wrestled with the problem of reconciling science with religion, for them the problem of their day, and in the great period of German idealism, between Lessing and Hegel, went far towards reaching a synthesis which aimed at preserving the essential meaning of protestant Christianity, without doing violence to modern rational convictions. The highest merit of classical German literature lies in its expression in new symbols of this humanistic religion.[12]

What Bruford's fine analysis does not mention, however, is that this new wine had to be poured into old, if relabeled, wineskins. It was all very well to leave the church for literature, but in eighteenth-century Germany literature paid no stipends. The ex-theologian could preach a new gospel, but he could not create for himself a new socioeconomic niche. He had, in material terms, to remain a clergyman, even if under some other name. He had, that is, to remain a member of the university-educated official intelligentsia, with special responsibility for the moral and psychological health of the nation, if he wished to retain an audience and a living. The great transformation which Schöffler described could not take place without a great cost in mental anguish and even physical suffering, for it required a redefinition of self and career in circumstances which allowed of very few alternatives. Within the social structure of the absolutist semi-feudal *Ständestaat*—the "state of estates" (i.e., castes)—the possibilities of escape were limited. Commercial success as a freelance was possible only for a writer who spoke for the true bourgeoisie and not for the "mixed noble-bourgeois stratum" of *die Gebildeten*—although it was they alone who had access to power and an effective national consciousness, albeit via the detour of compromise with absolutism. By about 1800 commercial success was just about possible for German writers, provided they confined themselves to the trivia with which alone their politically powerless audience was allowed to concern itself. So the only opening for an ex-theologian, if he was fortunate, and if he still wished to devote his intellect to the most serious national concerns, was some post as a salaried official.

That usually meant a professorship in one of the new university subjects being founded by others in a like position to himself: philosophy, history, or classical philology. In such a post his theological radicalism could be concealed, and though any political radicalism could be only indirectly expressed, he could enjoy security, a position of authority, and the attention of the administrative élite. Otherwise he was banished into the marginal role of a private tutor, unless, that is, he was prepared to give up his secularized mission to the nation or to pursue it as a kind of hobby on the side. But anyone who, like Kleist, wanted both to function as a political "preceptor of the nation" and to enjoy the economic and social independence that only the capitalist free market can provide was doomed from the start. If even Klopstock drew only 17 percent of his total income from his earnings as a writer, there was no hope for the lower-profile figure who wanted both to detach himself from a more or less overtly official career and to avoid selling himself body and soul to Grub Street.[13] Hence the tragically short creative careers in which German literature of this period is so rich—Lenz, Hölderlin, Kleist, Grabbe, even to some extent Schiller.

Those who avoided that fate, and even to some extent those who did not, contributed to the definition of a new range of intellectual and existential possibilities: a new humanistic theology and a new humanistic priesthood for the new humanistic religion. These new possibilities, however, retained the essential sociopolitical characteristics of their Christian and clerical predecessors; however novel the content, they remained modes of existence for *die Gebildeten*, the state-dependent intelligentsia, trained for their role in the universities. Under the new labels, the old functions continued. I shall mention three principal features of classical German culture, which can be regarded as secular continuations of the tasks of the pastorate.

In the first place, and most obviously, there was the teaching of philosophy, particularly post-Kantian idealist philosophy, the alternative career adopted not only by such famous ex-theologians as Reinhold, Hegel, and Schelling, but also by many other now forgotten former clergy in the period of the French Revolution. Indeed, the continuity with the preaching role of the pastor was sometimes so close that there seems little point in calling it anything else. In his 1794 lectures *On the Vocation of the Scholar*, Fichte proved to his hearers that in so far as they were Fichtean philosophers they had necessarily to be morally the best people of their age. The claim of philosophy to succeed and supplant theology is most explicit in Hegel's mature system, in which philosophy appears as the supreme manifestation of the Absolute, surpassing Art and Religion, at least for the educated élite. But in 1794 Fichte had already formulated with uncompromising clarity the demand of the new philosophy—it would be difficult to make such a claim on behalf of the thought of Locke or Hume—to displace the old clergy and to take over both their status and their stipends. "I am a priest of Truth," he announced in *On the Vocation of the Scholar*, "I am in her pay," though he did not add that the duke of Weimar was Truth's cashier.[14]

A second successor to the religion of the official pastorate was provided by the obsession with all things Greek.[15] Only in Germany did the Grecian thread in eighteenth-century taste acquire the intensity of an ideology. The emotional intensity is accounted for by the function the image of ancient Greece was required to perform as a counterexample to Christianity, the detachment from which had brought about the intellectual and existential crisis of the ex-pastor in the first place. It is the image of a world in which such a crisis does not need to occur. In that ancient world, at its peak in Periclean Athens, the human was not separated from the divine by the gulf of faith (and so of doubt), because the human, social, and natural world was itself understood as divine. In Schiller's words in *The Gods of Greece*, a hymn of hate against Christianity first published in 1788: "Da die Götter menschlicher noch waren Waren Menschen göttlicher" ("When the gods were more human, human beings were more godlike").[16] Similarly, the poets, sculptors, and architects who made the divine manifest in human words and artifacts, were—it is alleged—at one with the society whose divine dimension they celebrated. They were respected as vessels of a holy truth, acknowledged without difficulty by all; they were not as modern clergy are, either pharisaical prelates of an established but incredible religion or lonely and impoverished outcasts devoted to ideals their fellow-citizens cannot understand. This vision of ancient Greece as a world of perfect human fulfillment, in which society was at one with God, nature, and itself, and the poet was at one with society, both tormented Hölderlin and was the foundation for his greatest poems, expressions of eschatological yearning unsurpassed in modern literature. In pursuit of this vision Winckelmann turned his back on Germany and its anguished Protestant clergy, underwent a conversion to Catholicism, which conveniently enabled him to become secretary to a cardinal, and exiled himself to the great art collections of Rome, of which his impassioned descriptions inspired German eighteenth- and nineteenth-century artists, poets, and architects, and academics in at least three disciplines: classical philology, archaeology, and the history of the visual arts.

A third secular transformation of theology, after the preaching of secular wisdom and the construction of a pagan Greek utopia, and one which offered career possibilities outside the university, if not outside officialdom, was what we may call the invention of "Art." More is at issue here than the rise of aesthetics, though it is important to remember that the term "aesthetics," and the branch of philosophy which it describes, are creations of the eighteenth-century German university. When Alexander Gottlieb Baumgarten gave the term to the world in 1735, his intention was to show that there was a perfection proper to what the Leibnizians called clear but confused perceptions—that is, to the perceptions of the senses, the perfection, namely, traditionally called beauty.[17] The perfection of sensuous knowledge, therefore, did not lie in its ceasing to be confused, in its rising to become the distinct perceptions of logic and ultimately of theology. Its perfection was to be beautiful, and that was enough. This was more than an assertion that beauty was something different from intellectual perspicuousness, moral goodness, or theological truth. No doubt it was that too, and that was certainly a fateful step. But it was also an assertion that the study of beauty was a separate philosophical discipline, which could not be reduced to others, and which required its own place in the curriculum, its own professors, and ultimately its own endowments. Baumgarten was a pious man in holy orders, but in defining his new subject he was clearing a path for those who were neither. When in 1762 J. G. Hamann, the only truly independent critic of the German Enlightenment, published his *Aesthetica in nuce* (*All Aesthetics in a Nutshell*), his purpose was not to found an aesthetics of his own, but to anathematize the entire new burgeoning science of beauty as a cloak for secularization, a device for the surreptitious dethronement of the queen of the sciences, theology.[18]

What I have called the invention of "art," however, is not identical with the rise of aesthetics, though it runs in parallel with it. I am referring to a particular use of the word "art," in the singular, as a generic term, and with a metaphysical edge to it. Not "art" in the sense of "craft," in which sense it has a plural—the "fine arts," for example—the only sense known to Dr. Johnson, who in his *Dictionary* gives as an instance "the art of boiling sugar." "Art" in the sense which Oscar Wilde meant when he remarked that "all art is quite useless" is something of a novelty in the English language—Wilde's remark certainly does not apply to the Johnsonian art of jam-making. It is no doubt a nineteenth-century importation from Germany, where Wilde's concepts were elaborated a hundred years before him. In 1774, J. G. Sulzer, author of the encyclopaedic *General Theory of the Fine Arts,* did not know the usage, but in 1817 there was nothing terminologically innovative about Hegel's equation of Art with Religion and Philosophy as forms of absolute knowledge. Already in 1798, in the prologue to his play *Wallenstein*, Schiller refers to art as a phenomenon commensurate with life itself: "Ernst ist das Leben, heiter ist die Kunst" ("Life is earnest, Art serene"), and he, like Wilde, is plainly not thinking of jam.[19] How did it come about that in eighteenth-century Germany the word "art" (*Kunst*) acquired this status, at once comprehensive and portentous, almost sacred?

There are two aspects of the term that need to be explained. First, there is the epistemological aspect: the status of the activity and the products of "art" as a special means of knowing and representing all that is. Second, there is the comprehensiveness of "art": its reduction of all the fine arts to a single principle, and in particular its absorption of literature.

The question of the epistemological status of "art" is important for our theme because it is through the development of an idealist theory of knowledge that the concept comes to be most closely associated with secularized religion. There was of course a long tradition, reaching back through the Italian Renaissance to antiquity, and mediated to eighteenth-century Germany particularly by Shaftesbury, which saw the poet and the visual artist as divinely inspired and even as a second Maker or Creator, a just Prometheus under Jove. But I believe it was in the development of aesthetics in German eighteenth-century universities that the crucial step was taken of transferring the religious metaphors from the maker to the thing made and so building a vocabulary in which it was possible to speak not just of a divine Artist but of divine Art. Once again it is in Baumgarten that we find the modest but fateful innovation. The poet in his view makes or feigns worlds other than the real one, the one which the Leibnizian God has actually chosen to create, but these other worlds are rationally as plausible and possible as the real one.[20]

In the 1770s the literary revolutionaries of the Storm and Stress movement, for whom Sulzer's *General Theory of the Fine Arts* was obsolete pedantry, elaborated a view of the "creative genius"—both of them words which thenceforth became inseparable from aesthetic discussion—which took Baumgarten's discrete theological allusions to an extreme. The language of "creation" and "creativity" is extended from the artist to the work of art. Shakespeare is for Herder a "dramatic God," and Shakespeare's works similarly become susceptible of description in terms of a theologically tinged epistemology. They are "A world of dramatic history, as much and as profound as nature; yet its creator gives us the eyes and the point of view to see as much and as profoundly."[21] For Karl Philipp Moritz, a late systematizer of Storm and Stress aesthetics, Nature was identical with God and so the only true and personal creator was what he called "the artist." In a treatise which emerged from his conversations with Goethe in Rome in 1787, Moritz gives special attention to what he calls the "totality" of the work of art, its autonomy, its uselessness, as he calls it, that is, its freedom from any purpose extraneous to itself. In this totality Moritz sees the essential similarity between the work of art and the cosmos which it imitates. "Every beautiful whole" created by an artist bears, he writes, the imprint of "the great whole" that "is Nature."[22]

Soon after his meeting with Goethe, Moritz began lecturing in Berlin, where he was a close acquaintance of Marcus Herz, Kant's correspondent. It is unclear whether Moritz's thoughts on the uselessness of works of art stimulated Kant to reconsider the question of judgments of taste or whether, as is perhaps more likely, the current flowed in the opposite direction. In any event, Kant's *Critique of Judgment*, which appeared in 1790, had a similar program to his previous two critiques. It combined a synthesis of all the major concepts of eighteenth-century aesthetics with a relentless critique of their epistemological basis. It seemed therefore to cut off the path to the pantheistic theological aesthetic which was the natural culmination of much eighteenth-century German thought and which was sketched out in Moritz's treatise. However, as in the other areas of philosophy, Kant's criticisms were not listened to by his German contemporaries, and only the reconstructive and systematic elements in his work were allowed to stand. The development which *The Critique of Judgment* ought definitively to have interrupted resumed shortly afterwards and with renewed vigor. In the field of aesthetics, the man who turned the locomotive round, who turned what Kant had intended as a limitation on the moral and theological pretensions of the new science of beauty, into the basis for a newly grand expansion of its claims, and who at last gave to the term "art" its central position, was Schiller.

Schiller had long believed in the cultural mission of the poet, especially the dramatic poet, and when he met Moritz in 1788 and talked to him about his treatise he was writing a long didactic poem, *The Artists*, about the civilizing role throughout history of those preachers and practitioners of human order and harmony, a counterimage to the picture of theological decline he had painted in *The Gods of Greece*. In the philosophical treatises he then wrote under the impress of his reading of Kant, Schiller effectively undid the critical work of Kant's system while retaining its epistemological basis. Beauty, he announced, is freedom in appearance.[23] Fatefully, this near-identification of the moral and the beautiful—wholly alien to Kant—leaves no room for a separate theory of nonhuman, that is, natural beauty. Schiller's aesthetics becomes almost exclusively an aesthetics of art. In the experience of artistic beauty the experiencer is brought closer to the realization of that ideal humanity which for Schiller takes the place of the Leibnizian or any other divinity. The Kantian epistemological, or at any rate psychological, terms have been retained, importantly modified at certain points by Fichte, but the theological impetus of mid-eighteenth-century aesthetics has been restored, and of this moralized and secularized theology the concept of art has become a central pillar.

Schiller's influence on the younger generation, particularly the Tübingen group of Hölderlin, Hegel, and Schelling, was immediate, profound, and long-lasting. In a paper probably delivered by Hegel to a revolutionary club in Frankfurt in 1797 and now known as *The Oldest Systematic Program of German Idealism,* the belief is proclaimed that "the highest act of reason is an aesthetic act," and it is announced that the author's projected philosophical system, which is to include physics, ethics, politics, and religion, will be unified by the supreme "Idea of Beauty."[24] The slightly younger triad of Romantic thinkers, Friedrich Schlegel, Novalis, and Schleiermacher, who ridiculed Schiller but could not escape his ideas, tried a somewhat different rearrangement of the same elements—idealist epistemology, aesthetics, and religion—by seeking to reverse the dissolution of theology into philosophy and aesthetics and to recombine idealism and art into a new religion. "I am thinking of founding a new religion," Schlegel remarked in 1798, "what else results from the synthesis of Goethe and Fichte [that is, of poetry and philosophy] but religion?"[25] Schelling, who linked both groups, may be said to have achieved the philosophical canonization of "art"—its definitive recognition as a distinct and unified activity of the mind deserving the most serious attention—in his *System of Transcendental Idealism,* published at the end of 1800. Schelling's philosophy as a whole was conceived as consisting of two branches, a philosophy of nature and a philosophy of spirit. The philosophy of spirit, to which *The System of Transcendental Idealism* is devoted, passes through the several philosophies of mind, ethics, and history to culminate in the philosophy of art. "Art" then unifies both branches of philosophy. "Art is the highest there is for the philosopher," Schelling writes, "because it so to speak opens up to him the Holy of Holies, where that which is sundered in Nature and History burns as it were in a single flame in eternal and original unity."[26] The former theologian, probably still technically an atheist, speaks again the language of his seminary years.

In a series of lectures (*Lectures on the Method of Academic Study*) delivered in 1802, Schelling offers a conspectus of the new disciplines that have developed in the last quarter of a century in the form of a redefinition of the academic curriculum in the terms of idealist philosophy. Seen in these terms there is an intimate link between them all: history (especially history of the transition from classical antiquity to Christian modernity), theology (which as Christian theology is necessarily historical), philosophy, and the theory of art are all aspects of the same absolute knowledge, all of them requiring to be taught and studied, and so—we might add in the light of our previous reflections—all requiring their endowed chairs. Pride of place, however, at the summit of the work goes to aesthetics and its reciprocal relation with philosophy, of which it shows "the inner essence . . . as in a magical or symbolical mirror." And Schelling concludes with an admonition to princes to support "art" (*die Kunst*) as a "necessary and integrating part of a state constitution formulated in accordance with Idealist principles." To that they should feel spurred by the example of antiquity in which "all . . . festivals . . . monuments, dramas . . . were only the different branches of a single general objective and living work of art."[27]

The second aspect of the ideology of "art" to which I referred was the comprehensiveness of the neologism "art," its reduction of "the arts" to a single principle, and its absorption of literature. *Les Beaux-Arts réduits à un même principe* is the title of Abbé Charles Batteux's treatise, published in 1746, which may count as the high point of the theory of *ut pictura poesis*—poetry and painting are and should be alike because like all the fine arts they have in common that in different media they imitate, or make pictures of, nature. The notion of imitation, however, is not the most important feature of the theory for our present purposes, but the theory's systematic and unifying intent. Now, in Europe at large, *ut pictura poesis* may indeed have reached its high point in the first half of the eighteenth century, but by the end of the second half it was largely defunct. It survived, however, in a reduced and subterranean form in the singular German concept of "Art"—for the belief that the different arts are different applications of a single principle survives in the presumption that all belong in the same metaphysical category of "die Kunst." Indeed the link with the *ut pictura poesis* school can be seen explicitly in the most aesthetic of the German idealist systems, that of Schopenhauer, for whom the entire field of art is simply the second form of the world as representation.

The principal reason for the collapse of the *ut pictura poesis* theory in the world beyond German philosophy was, I believe, the increasing independence and changing nature of literature as modern mass-publishing came into existence and with it new genres, notably the periodical, including the newspaper, and the novel. Literature became so different that it made no sense to try to bring it under the same heading as other activities. Literature had always been a craft, but it was never obviously one of the fine arts, except perhaps as poetry, and not all of poetry at that. Sociologically speaking, the unifying characteristic of the fine arts in early-eighteenth-century Europe—painting, sculpture, architecture, orchestral music, opera, and even much nonmusical drama—was that in order to be practiced they required wealthy patrons. In Germany, at least, that meant they required princes, sovereigns who would subsidize them out of state funds, provide pensions for artists so they could study abroad, for example, or make large annual grants to theaters, maintain orchestras, or build and gild palaces. By contrast literature, even in Germany, and certainly elsewhere in Europe in the eighteenth century, was increasingly a middle-class and commercial affair. By the end of the century, as I have remarked, it was possible to earn an independent bourgeois living as a writer of sorts. The problem in Germany was that, as a member of the independent bourgeoisie, you were cut off from the political élite, the official class; you had nothing important to write about and no one important to write for. It is not surprising that many of Germany's earliest successful writers for money were women. Aesthetics was created as a discipline, and philosophy was almost exclusively written, by members of that male, noncommercial, political élite, that state-dependent officialdom. Their incorporation of literature into "art" was a preemptive strike against any claim to cultural, and ultimately political, autonomy by commercial writers. Literature had to be defined into conformity with other crafts whose practitioners were unambiguously dependent on the prince's funding and were loyal to him. Throughout the nineteenth century in Germany the distinction was maintained between the "Dichter," or poet, the author of literature as "art," who, directly or indirectly, was maintained by the state, and the "Schriftsteller," or writer, who sold his work for money.

I have promised a few words on an American context in which to see these matters, and they will have to be very few. Frederic Henry Hedge, Harvard's first professor of German literature, remarked in 1833 that "the preeminence of Germany among the nations of our day in respect of intellectual culture is universally acknowledged; and we do fully believe that whatever excellence that nation has attained in science, in history, or poetry is mainly owing to the influence of her philosophy. . . . In theology this influence has been most conspicuous."[28] Certainly it is difficult to imagine the intellectual history of any of the English-speaking countries in the nineteenth century without the influence of "the infidel philosophers and theologians of Germany," as Andrews Norton, dictator of the Harvard Divinity School, notoriously described them in 1839.[29] In particular the situation of Harvard Unitarian clergy in the 1820s and 1830s had close similarities with that of the German clergy half a century and more before, and it was natural enough that German writings should speak to their condition. As philosophical and biblical doubts alienated them from the religion and the institutions in which they had been educated, they looked around for a new social role and in some cases a new livelihood. After study in Göttingen and a consultation with Goethe, William Emerson gave up theology for law and a career on Wall Street. His younger brother, Ralph Waldo, found in Goethe "the restorer of Faith and Love after the desolation of Hume and the French . . . he married Faith and Reason for the world" and less than a month after writing these words in 1832 gave up his clerical ministry.[30] After returning from Europe the following year, he drew from Hedge's article the inspiration to concern himself with German thought, in which Hedge was a guide to him as to many others, including Margaret Fuller, Theodore Parker, and George Ripley. Parker, who read Schelling's *Lectures on the Method of Academic Study* along with much other German philosophy while he was studying divinity at Harvard, of course remained in his orders—rather like Herder, one is tempted to say—but in the balance of his activities he shifted in the same direction as those who took the more radical step.[31]

For Emerson, Ripley, and others, lecturing and journalism and social utopianism took the place of sermons and tracts and hermeneutical speculations. The movement of transcendentalism was born in New England, rather as idealism, classicism, and romanticism arose in Germany, out of the spiritual and to some extent the material needs of a clergy with doubts, and of course it was from the Kantian philosophy that Hedge's Transcendental Club took its name. However, as the example of William Emerson clearly shows, there was a crucial difference between American and German circumstances: economic opportunity and the separation of church and state meant that in America alternative careers for the ex-theologian did exist, and even if, like William's younger brother, he continued in such postclerical activities as lecturing and morally edifying writing, he did not have to find a niche in the state bureaucracy in order to do so.

As a result, something of the intellectual intensity and existential anguish of the German writers is missing in their American counterparts, and in particular the ideology of pure "art," so integral a part of the self-definition of German officialdom, made little headway. The collision of American and German traditions, and the difficulty of reconciling them, can be felt at that odd moment in *Walden* when Thoreau, having insisted so emphatically on his economic and personal self-sufficiency, is suddenly brought, by his discussion of reading Homer, to address issues of what he calls "collective" policy for which nothing he has so far written has prepared us.

> It is time that villages were universities. . . . Shall the world be confined to one Paris or one Oxford forever? Cannot students be boarded here and get a liberal education under the skies of Concord? . . . In this country the village should in some respects take the place of the nobleman of Europe. It should be the patron of the fine arts. . . . As the nobleman of cultivated taste surrounds himself with whatever conduces to his culture,—genius—learning—wit—books— paintings—statuary—music—philosophical instruments, and the like, so let the village do. . . . New England can hire all the wise men in the world to come and teach her . . . and not be provincial at all.[32]

What on earth is this European nobleman, dragging behind him all the paraphernalia of some Schloss or palazzo, doing on the shores of Walden Pond? He is, I think, the emblem or symptom of an incongruity which Thoreau instinctively recognizes between two factors determining his own attitudes. On the one hand there is "the village," the native society of self-made Jeffersonian men, whose independence he has been taking to that extreme point at which it almost equates to detachment from society altogether. On the other hand there is the secular culture fostered in universities which are the organs of very differently structured states, hierarchical, authoritarian, even absolutist, and that secular culture is essential to the intellectual survival of the men whom Thoreau most admires, the ex-clergy of whom Emerson his mentor is surely the supreme example. Thoreau does not himself belong to that group but he deeply sympathizes with it, and so he can give particularly vivid and half-voluntarily satirical expression to its collision with an American world. Imagining a village university, he is carried on by his sardonic intelligence to the consequential image of a nobleman in Concord.

"Art" in the pure sense—"art for art's sake" and so as a substitute religion—could never become the driving force in American literary culture because it was, in its German origins, the product of a quite desperate social and economic constriction. None of the great German philosophers and writers who contributed to forming that concept had the social mobility and freedom of action of an Emerson. In the American context only women came close to knowing the constraints which gave birth to "art," and among the transcendentalists it was probably Margaret Fuller who most faithfully transmitted the concept to an American public. Though the term she used for preference was "poesy," borrowed from Schlegel and Novalis, it also plainly owed quite as much to Schiller, whose poem *The Artists* was part of the twenty-four-week crash-course which Fuller ran in the German language.[33] "In their essence and their end," she says, poesy and religion "are one," and poesy is "the ground of the true art of life; it being not merely truth, not merely good, but the beauty which integrates both."[34] That integrative and so higher function accorded to beauty aligns Fuller as much with Schelling and Schiller as with Emerson, the members of whose trinity of Truth, Beauty, and Goodness are all on an equal footing. In American circumstances literature rarely needed to call forth so explicitly religious a passion as animated Schiller, Schelling, Hölderlin, or the early Romantics, and where it did, as far as I can judge, the American tradition of religious liberty and diversity was so strong that it appeared more as the idiosyncratic enthusiasm of a sectary or social reformer than as the inescapable commitment of a whole class. For Denton Snider, the literary mainstay of the St. Louis Hegelian movement, which brought a modified form of transcendentalism to the Midwest, Homer, Dante, Shakespeare, and Goethe were the "four Bibles" to the exposition of which he devoted many volumes and a lifetime of proselytizing.[35] Snider's literary "schools," as he called them, parallel and linked to the Concord School of Philosophy, may have been only simulacra of universities—village universities, perhaps. But through the Great Books tradition, which he certainly influenced, the belief that the universality of literature transcends the particularities of religion has become received wisdom in universities throughout the English-speaking world.

Am I then saying that literature conceived as "art," or produced under the influence of that conception, is some crypto-Protestant or crypto-Spinozan by-product of secularist bureaucracy which no good Catholic faculty, let alone in a free country and a liberal economy, should touch with a barge-pole? Not at all (or not entirely). What I am saying is that we cannot read literature with a sense of the theological implications of what we are doing and reading—which is how C. S. Lewis always strove to read—without also having a sense of the social and historical origins of the terms we are using and the texts to which we are applying them, and that that social and historical understanding has to be part of our theology in the first place. If our Catholicism is big enough and discerning enough to see the working of divine grace in the Protestant Reformation and its consequences, then we shall be able to read the classical and romantic literature and philosophy of Germany, which has had so great a role in shaping our modern world, with understanding and profit. But the same social and historical analysis which reveals the roots of that literature in a crisis of Protestantism also reveals its particularity, its determination by specific local and historical circumstances, and its divergence from the much broader current of European and Atlantic literature since the Reformation. We see, for example, that the bureaucratic and elitist quality of German culture in this period distances it from the literature produced for the new large-scale commercial publishing market, above all from the novel, the form in which nineteenth-century and twentieth-century literature in English, French, Italian, Spanish, and Russian has most notably succeeded in representing the world which God has created and in which His redemption is active. We see that whereas in Germany the quasi-philosophical language of aesthetics dominated a literary discussion which was largely academic, elsewhere a more public discussion in widely-circulated journals was based on the premise that literary criticism was in the end a more or less subtle form of moral criticism. Indeed, only if we recognize what is specifically different about the German tradition will we begin to understand the complex nature of those great American achievements of the nineteenth century which resulted from the intimate symbiosis of German and Anglo-Saxon elements, the work of Whitman and Melville, for example.

I should like therefore to conclude with three thoughts about a major twentieth-century attempt to bring together Catholic theology and the study of literature, the work of Hans Urs von Balthasar, or rather, since I have not read more than a small fraction of his enormous oeuvre, volume three, part one, of *Herrlichkeit* (*The Glory of the Lord*), itself a treatise of 983 pages.

My first thought concerns a problem of method. The subtitle of *Herrlichkeit* as a whole is *Eine theologische Ästhetik* (*A Theological Aesthetics*). All the principal terms Balthasar uses to conduct his investigation—"aesthetics," "Art," "the beautiful"—derive from, or are profoundly influenced by, the usage of the German classical and romantic, or idealist, generations. Heidegger, for example, if using such terms, would have introduced them with at least twenty pages of reflective wordplay centered on their real or imagined etymology. Balthasar, however—who was a "Germanist," an academic student of German literature, before he became a theologian—seems quite uncritical in his approach. He applies the word "aesthetics" to Greek, Jewish, or patristic texts without reflecting on the eighteenth-century Leibnizian context in which it originated.[36] He calls his subject-matter "Kunst Gottes," "God's art," without noting that "art" in this sense is a more recent neologism even than "aesthetics."[37] And "beauty" he refuses to define at all, since those who claim not to know what it is are more certainly beyond redemption than those who claim not to know what is true or what is good.[38] "Beauty," he says, "is our first word," and he aims to restore Beauty to its proper place beside Truth and Goodness—though he seems not to notice that many a nineteenth-century thinker before him, including Emerson, had sought to do the same.[39] In his understanding of "aesthetics," "Art," and "beauty," Balthasar is, as much as the nineteenth-century sages, the inheritor of the secular gospels of ex-clergymen. The parallels with Emerson and Margaret Fuller are not fortuitous. Indeed there is a strong likeness to the case of Orestes Brownson, who similarly defended himself against the temptations of transcendentalism by recourse to supernaturalism, a dualism of nature and supernature like that which everywhere undergirds Balthasar's system.

There is an acute danger of tautology when Balthasar sets about giving a historical structure to his argument, as he does in *Herrlichkeit* III/1. That argument, reduced from 983 pages to ten lines, is that New Testament Christianity brought together the Greek experience of the Divine as beauty and the Jewish revelation of the Divine as glory.[40] That amalgamation of beauty and glory was broken apart at the Reformation by Luther,[41] who insisted on God's unadulterated and unapproachable glory, leaving those who remained outside the Catholic church to pursue theological beauty either through an attempted return to Greek antiquity or through the development of a purely humanistic metaphysics.[42] These two alternative movements of post-Reformation secularity culminate in the Promethean attempt of German idealism to combine them both, and after the tragic collapse of that hubristic structure modern humanity is left with nothing but soulless materialism.

Now we have seen that the obsession with Greek antiquity and the urge to develop a secular metaphysics, and indeed the invention of aesthetics itself, are all features of Protestant German culture in its classic and romantic or idealist phase, deriving from the secularization of its clerical class. The problem of method to which I have alluded is that it is difficult to determine whether this cultural moment in Germany around 1800 genuinely represents, as Balthasar claims, the culmination of a two-thousand-year-long clash of the fundamental forces in Christian intellectual history; or whether, rather, since Balthasar has from the start defined the forces in German idealist terms, it is inevitable that these forces and their conflict should be most clearly and decisively expressed in the philosophy and literature of secularizing German idealism. Perhaps even Balthasar's understanding of the Jewish revelation of divine glory is only a reading back into the Old Testament of what he believes Luther to have stood for. In that case the entire Greek-Jewish opposition and synthesis would be suspiciously homologous with the internal tensions in the intellectual life of late-eighteenth-century Germany. Is the structure of this part of *Herrlichkeit* all a great hermeneutical circle, Balthasar first reading his own intellectual and cultural ambience into the past and then finding his own views confirmed by what the past tells him? The matter could only really be decided if we could point to some unquestionably major feature of the Western intellectual and literary tradition of which both Balthasar and German idealism are unable to give a serious account, and that for reasons which in the case of German idealism are clearly connected not with the intellectual coherence but with the social and historical determinants of the movement.

My second thought about Balthasar, then, is that there does indeed seem to be such a lacuna in his coverage and his sensibility, and this is of great importance if we wish to take him as a guide through that difficult terrain in which literature and theology intermingle. I have already remarked that German literature of the idealist period is marked by a disdain for the developing mass-market in publishing and for the new genre which particularly sustains it, the realistic novel. A similar disdain is to be found in Balthasar. Indeed, so breathtaking is the snobbery of the Germanist-turned-clergyman in the few lines that in all his great work he devotes to the principal literary form of the last three centuries that I really have to quote them, even if abbreviated:

> that broad, dull stratum of inner-worldly, almost religionless "cultural humanism" . . . floods the field of art [we note the word] in the novel of bourgeois realism: from Scott to Dickens, Thackeray, Galsworthy [but there is no mention of George Eliot, Melville, James, Conrad, Lawrence], from Freytag and Keller to Fontane and Thomas Mann [and Kafka?], from Balzac through Stendhal and Flaubert to Zola, from Pushkin to Tolstoy and Hamsun—all the time it is man in his milieu, environment, nature, cosmos, growing into them or growing out of them, explicating or complicating himself . . . [the novel

represents] the self-dissolution of immanent anthropology that in its closed logic has increasing recourse to perversion to arouse any kind of excitement.[43]

There is much that could be said about this passage, and about the similarity of its critical arguments to those advanced against modern literature and art in the 1920s and '30s by sympathizers with National Socialism such as Heidegger and Ernst Jünger. It is clear that for Balthasar novelists are *Schriftsteller*, not *Dichter*. But I will make only one potentially theological point: even if this characterization of modern realistic prose were correct—and it is blatantly untrue—that body of literature should still be of the greatest interest to a theological aesthetics for the fullness of its depiction of a world so interesting to God that He sent His Son to redeem it.

That brings me to my third thought. Fifteen years before *Herrlichkeit* III/1 there was published a study of almost exactly the same range of Western literary culture, from Homer and the Old Testament to Virginia Woolf, which also has a distinctive theological thesis underlying it. It too was written by a German scholar, though a scholar of the Romance languages. Universal in its sympathies where Balthasar is parochial, passionately engaged with literature and the business of criticism rather than with the art and aesthetics of a bureaucratic élite, Erich Auerbach's *Mimesis: The Representation of Reality in Western Literature* is not mentioned in any of Balthasar's volumes which I have consulted. Yet Auerbach's thesis that Western literary realism has been made possible by the combination in the Gospels of a Jewish-Christian typological substructure with what the ancients knew as the "low style," the *genus humile dicendi*, is of direct relevance to what is or ought to be Balthasar's central theme—the manifestation in the flesh of the glory as of the only-begotten of the Father. Balthasar's aesthetics cannot remain faithful to that central Christological principle—that the Word was made flesh and dwelt amongst us—because he has only dualistic supernaturalism to protect him against the magnetic power of his idealist antecedents. For Auerbach's realist approach, such issues never arise: the glory is already there in the humility, and beauty has no part in the story.

Balthasar, however, has little interest in the low style, the style which notices that Peter was warming himself at a fire while denying Christ. Indeed, when in his *Theodramatik* Balthasar comes to deal with what ought to be one of the high points of all literature for a theological aesthetics, the late medieval cycles of mystery plays, he passes over them quickly with expressions of regret at the intrusion of unseemly and comic elements into the sacred action and at the involvement of lay people in what ought to be the preserve of the priests.[44] It is a telling contrast that when medieval romance is being discussed Balthasar deals with Wolfram von Eschenbach and Auerbach with Chrétien de Troyes. Balthasar chooses Wolfram's version of the Parsifal legend because, he says, theological issues are explicit in it, whereas the version by Chrétien merely tells a good story.[45] Auerbach of course selects Chrétien because unless a theology of literature can explain to us what are the theological implications of telling a good story, it is not a theology of literature at all, but merely theology using literary examples. Altogether it is striking how different the Western canon appears in two works which, under one aspect at least, have such similar goals. Auerbach only once deals with a German writer, and even though I am by profession concerned for the merits, however peculiar, of German literature, I would have to say that Auerbach's selection corresponds more nearly to most people's perception of what Western literature is, at any rate in the Romance and English-speaking world.

However, I do not wish to give the wrong impression. Balthasar's theology is for others to judge, but even in the realm of his aesthetics I would not wish to be thought to be saying that there is nothing of value in his undertaking. On the contrary, I think it of central importance to the study of literature, above all in a Catholic university, that we should reflect on its relation to the study of theology—whether we approach that relation as a historical and social issue, as I have mainly been suggesting, or whether we approach it as an issue in the theory of narrative discourse, of which Auerbach's book could be seen as a first sketch. If Balthasar's application of a German idealist schema to Christian intellectual history is unpersuasive, he is a highly intelligent critic of the German tradition itself. Many jewels can be found in the mud of his prose, as when he remarks that in Christian literature as a whole comedy predominates over tragedy—a sentiment which brings him close to Auerbach. He then links this to some fine comments on Shakespeare and the English novel—and adds with admirable South-Germanic patriotism that in Austria "with Mozart, Raimund, Nestroy, Hofmannsthal Christian light triumphs over hollow German earnestness."[46] If I regret that Balthasar has not developed this delightful point further, and certainly not applied it to his own treatise, that may simply be because, for historical and social reasons which I cannot fully discern, I share C. S. Lewis's prejudice in favor of literature and criticism rather than art and aesthetics.

NOTES

1. Eda Sagarra, *A Social History of Germany, 1648–1914* (London: Methuen, 1977), 82.

2. Rudolf Vierhaus, *Deutschland im Zeitalter des Absolutismus (1648–1763)*, Deutsche Geschichte, 6 (Göttingen: Vanderhoeck and Ruprecht, 1978), 78. Cf. Hans Heinrich Gerth, *Bürgerliche Intelligenz um 1800: Zur Soziologie des deutschen Frühliberalismus*, Kritische Studien zur Geschichtswissenschaft, 19 (Göttingen: Vanderhoeck and Ruprecht, 1976), 44–45.

3. T. C. W. Blanning, *Reform and Revolution in Mainz, 1743–1803* (Cambridge: Cambridge University Press, 1974), 14.

4. "Adlig-bürgerlichen Mischschicht," see Wolfgang Zorn, "Deutsche Führungsschichten des 17. und 18. Jahrhunderts: Forschungsergebnisse seit 1945," *Internationales Archiv für Sozialgeschichte der deutschen Literatur* 6 (1981): 190.

5. Georg Wilhelm Friedrich Hegel, *Grundlinien der Philosophie des Rechts*, §205, in *Werke*, ed. Eva Moldenhauer and Karl Markus Michel, 20 vols. (Frankfurt: Suhrkamp, 1969–71), 7:357.

6. Zorn, "Führungsschichten," 191.

7. Gerth, *Bürgerliche Intelligenz*, 87; cf. Herbert Schöffler, "Anruf der Schweizer," in *Deutscher Geist im 18. Jahrhundert: Essays zur Geistes- und Religionsgeschichte*, 2d ed. (Göttingen: Vanderhoeck and Ruprecht, 1967), 7–60.

8. Sagarra, *Social History*, 119.

9. Herbert Schöffler, *Protestantismus und Literatur* (Leipzig: B. Tauchnitz, 1922), 228, cited in W. H. Bruford, *Theatre, Drama, and Audience in Goethe's Germany* (London: Routledge and Paul, 1950), 114.

10. Ibid.

11. Albert Ward, *Book Production, Fiction, and the German Reading Public, 1740–1800* (Oxford: Clarendon Press, 1974), 33, 164–65.

12. Bruford, *Theatre, Drama, and Audience*, 115.

13. Gerhard Sauder, "Sozialgeschichtliche Aspekte der Literatur im 18. Jahrhundert," *Internationales Archiv für Sozialgeschichte der deutschen Literatur* 4 (1979): 214.

14. J. G. Fichte, *Sämmtliche Werke* (repr. 1971; Berlin, 1845–46), 6:333.

15. Cf. Gerth, *Bürgerliche Intelligenz*, 43.

16. Friedrich Schiller, *Sämtliche Werke*, ed. Gerhard Fricke and Herbert G. Göpfert, 5 vols. (Munich: C. Hanser, 1965), 1:169.

17. Hans Reiss, "The Rise of Aesthetics from Baumgarten to Humboldt," in *The Cambridge History of Literary Criticism*, vol. 4, *The Eighteenth Century*, ed. H. B. Nisbet and Claude Rawson (Cambridge: Cambridge University Press, 1997), 658–80, 658–59.

18. As Hans Urs von Balthasar has claimed, *Herrlichkeit: Eine theologische Ästhetik*, 3 vols. (Einsiedeln: Johannes, 1961), 1:78.

19. Schiller, *Sämtliche Werke*, 2:274.

20. Alexander Gottlieb Baumgarten, *Reflections on Poetry*, ed. Karl Aschenbrenner and W. B. Holther (Berkeley and Los Angeles: University of California Press, 1954), scholium to §68.

21. J. G. Herder, *Sämtliche Werke*, ed. Bernhard Suphan, 33 vols. (Berlin, 1877–1913), 5:221.

22. K. P. Moritz, *Über die bildende Nachahmung des Schönen*, Deutsche Litteratur-denkmale des 18. und 19. Jahrhunderts, 31, ed. S. Auerbach (Heilbronn, 1888), 14.

23. Schiller, letter to C. G. Körner, 8 February 1793, *Schillers Werke*, vol. 26, ed. Edith Nahler and Horst Nahler (Weimar: H. Böhlaus Nachfolger, 1992), 183.

24. Hegel, *Werke*, 1:234–36.

25. Friedrich Schlegel, to Novalis, 2 December 1798, *Kritische Friedrich-Schlegel-Ausgabe*, ed. Ernst Behler et al., 3d ed., vol. 24 (Paderborn: F. Schöningh, 1985), 205.

26. F. W. J. Schelling, *Schriften von 1799–1801* (Darmstadt: Wissenschaftliche Buch-gesellschaft, 1975), 628.

27. F. W. J. Schelling, *Schriften von 1801–1804* (Darmstadt Wissenschaftliche Buch-gesellschaft, 1981), 586.

28. F. H. Hedge, "Coleridge's Literary Character—German Metaphysics," in *Selected Writings of the American Transcendentalists*, ed. George Hochfield (New York: New American Library, 1966), 119–27; the quotation appears at 127.

29. Andrews Norton, "A Discourse on the Latest Form of Infidelity" (1839), in ibid., 203–9; the quotation appears at 203.

30. Henry A. Pochmann, *German Culture in America: Philosophical and Literary Influences, 1600–1900* (Madison: University of Wisconsin Press, 1957), 169.

31. Ibid., 216.

32. H. D. Thoreau, *Walden: or, Life in the Woods*, in *Walden . . . and On the Duty of Civil Disobedience*, chapter 3, "Reading" (New York: New American Library, 1960), 78.

33. Pochmann, *German Culture*, 761.

34. Ibid., 441.

35. Ibid., 283.

36. Balthasar, *Herrlichkeit*, 1:47.

37. Ibid., 33.

38. Ibid., 18, 34.

39. Ibid., 16.

40. Ibid.

41. Ibid., 3.1:318–19.

42. Ibid., 593–94.

43. Ibid., 750–51.

44. Hans Urs von Balthasar, *Theodramatik*, 4 vols. (Einsiedeln: Johannes, 1973–83), 1:97.

45. Balthasar, *Herrlichkeit*, 3.1:503, n. 1; Erich Auerbach, *Mimesis: The Representation of Reality in Western Literature*, trans. Willard Trask (1953; New York: Doubleday Anchor Books, 1957), 107–24.

46. Balthasar, *Herrlichkeit*, 3.1:503–4.

6

Catholic Thought and Dilemmas of Human Rights

MARY ANN GLENDON

THE CONTRIBUTORS TO THIS VOLUME ON "HIGHER LEARNING AND Catholic Traditions" were invited to reflect on whether the Catholic intellectual heritage could offer "unexplored points of view and intellectual models" useful in our respective fields of study. In my case, that invitation arrived when I was in the midst of research on the framing of the United Nations' Universal Declaration of Human Rights (UDHR), and just at a point where I had concluded that Catholic thought might be helpful in resolving four thorny dilemmas that have beset the human rights project from its outset: the dilemmas arising from challenges to its universality, its foundations, its truth claims, and the indivisibility of fundamental rights.

The UDHR was drafted over a two-year period by the U.N.'s first Human Rights Commission, chaired by Eleanor Roosevelt, and was proclaimed by the General Assembly as a "common standard of achievement" in December 1948. Though the Great Powers of the day attached little importance to that aspirational document, the Universal Declaration surprised everyone by becoming the world's single most important reference point for cross-cultural discussions of human freedom and dignity. It became the polestar of humanity's second great "rights moment," the era of the rights instruments that may be called dignitarian, to distinguish them from their more libertarian eighteenth-century predecessors.[1]

For most of the twentieth century, Catholic social thought and the dignitarian vision of human rights have been closely connected. In this essay, I briefly review some of the ways in which Catholic thought influenced

the content of the UDHR, and the manner in which that "gift" was reciprocated when the church drew upon the Universal Declaration in its Vatican II documents and in several papal encyclicals. Then, turning to the
main subject of this volume, I suggest that it is time for the flow of ideas
to be reversed again as friends of human rights struggle to prevent the
Universal Declaration from being pulled apart and politicized beyond
recognition.

1. Catholic Influences on the Universal Declaration

Americans, when they read the Universal Declaration,[2] are apt to be struck
by its differences from, as well as its similarities to, our own Bill of Rights,
especially where its emphases on family protection and social and economic justice are concerned. Economic conservatives often surmise that
the rights to social security, to work, to protection against unemployment,
to join trade unions, and to an adequate standard of living were included
at the behest of the Soviet Union, and for that reason alone many have
refused to take the Declaration seriously as a universal standard.[3] Catholics
acquainted with the church's social doctrine, however, will find more than
a few familiar ideas: the emphasis on the "inherent dignity" and "worth
of the human person"; the affirmation that the human person is "endowed
with reason and conscience"; the recognition of the family as the "natural and fundamental group unit of society" entitled as such to "protection by society and the state"; the insistence that certain economic and
social goods are "indispensable" for human dignity; that parents have a
prior right to choose the education of their children; and that motherhood
and childhood are entitled to "special care and assistance."[4]

These concepts are not prominent in the Anglo-American rights tradition, but neither do they fit neatly with Marxist-Leninist rights theory,
which makes the state the sole source and guarantor of rights. Where,
then, did these ideas come from? In the manner of legal drafters everywhere, the framers of the UDHR derived most of the content of its thirty
articles from existing models—constitutions and rights instruments that
the staff of the U.N. Human Rights Division had collected from all over the
world.[5] The provisions listed above were based mainly on early twentieth-
century continental European and Latin American constitutions, and from
the document that became the 1948 Pan-American (or Bogota) Declaration of the Rights and Duties of Man. The ideas they embodied were stan-

dard features of the dignitarian family of rights instruments, and they are part of what sets that family apart both from positivist state socialism and the more individualistic, liberty-based constitutions of the Anglo-American world.[6]

But how did this constellation of ideas find its way into so many twentieth-century constitutions? The proximate answer to that question is mainly through the programs of political parties. The social and economic rights were promoted by Social-Democratic, Labour, and Christian parties alike, while rights pertaining to the family and the protection of the mediating structures of civil society were more attributable to Christian political and labor organizations.

But where did Christian parties and unions get *their* ideas about the family, work, civil society, and the dignity of the person? The proximate answer to that question is mainly from *Rerum Novarum* (1891) and *Quadragesimo Anno* (1931), in which Leo XIII and Pius XI, respectively, rethought the Enlightenment, the eighteenth-century revolutions, socialism, and the labor question in the light of Scripture, tradition, and the church's experience as an "expert in humanity."[7]

Even before World War II drew to a close, voices were raised in several quarters in favor of including some sort of human rights provision in an eventual peace treaty.[8] Among them was that of Pope Pius XII, who, in his 1 June 1941 radio address, called for an international bill recognizing the rights that flowed from the dignity of the person.[9] Against that background, it is easy to see how the dignitarian rights tradition found its way into many national legal systems and ultimately into the Universal Declaration.

Contrary to what is now widely believed, the UDHR's social and economic justice provisions also had very broad support—including from the United States until the Eisenhower administration reorganized the State Department and asked for Eleanor Roosevelt's resignation from the Human Rights Commission. (There were, to be sure, heated disputes over the precise formulation of those ideas and the manner in which they were to be implemented). The most zealous promoters of social and economic goods in the particular form in which they entered the Declaration were from the Latin American countries, then the largest single group of countries in the United Nations.

The family-related provisions also had broad support in the drafting process. They were already present in many Latin American and continental European constitutions, and were thus quite familiar to René Cassin, the French Jewish lawyer who was one of the chief drafters of the Declaration. It was Cassin who introduced most of this material into the draft, where it was expanded and refined by many others over a two-year period. The main defender of this group of ideas was Lebanon's Charles Malik, the most formidable intellectual on the drafting committee. I was struck, in reading U.N. records, to see Malik's use of terms like "intermediate associations" of civil society, and his emphatic preference for the term "person" rather than "individual." Later, I had the opportunity to ask Malik's son where his father, a member of the Greek Orthodox faith, had acquired his ideas about the social dimension of personhood and the importance of mediating structures. The answer was from *Rerum Novarum* and *Quadragesimo Anno*. Charles Malik was one of the first of an impressive line of non-Catholic intellectuals who have found a treasure trove of ideas in Catholic social teaching.

Besides those direct influences on the drafting process, there were several indirect channels through which Catholic thought reached the framers of the UDHR. The National Catholic Welfare Conference (forerunner of the National Conference of Catholic Bishops) had an observer at practically every session of the Human Rights Commission. And both Cassin and Malik were acquainted with Jacques Maritain, who was one of the most active members of a committee that UNESCO had appointed to study the theoretical foundations of human rights.

When the draft Declaration was submitted for one last review to a large committee composed of representatives from all fifty-eight U.N. member nations, the Latin Americans were again among the most active participants, offering many amendments and refinements. The Canadian lawyer who was then serving as the Director of the U.N. Division of Human Rights did not like this time-consuming development at all. In his memoirs, John Humphrey referred to the Latin American efforts to bring in ideas from the 1948 Pan-American Declaration as "the Bogota Menace." Of the group's Cuban spokesman, he said, "Highly intelligent, Guy Perez Cisneros used every procedural device to reach his end. His speeches were laced with Roman Catholic social philosophy, and it seemed at times that the chief protagonists in the conference room were the Roman Catholics and the communists, with the latter a poor second."[10] In his private diaries, Humphrey gave somewhat freer vent to his feelings. There, he described Cisneros as a man who "combines demagogy with Roman Catholic social philosophy," and said that the Cuban "should burn in hell" for holding up the proceedings with his numerous calls for amendments.[11] There were of course many other influences on the Universal Declaration, but as the foregoing discussion indicates, it is no mere coincidence that its implicit vision of personhood, its attention to the mediating structures of civil society, its dignitarian character, and its insistence on the links between freedom and social justice so closely resemble the social teachings of Leo XIII and Pius XI. In later years, that influence was reciprocated.

2. The Influence of the Universal Human Rights Idea on Catholic Social Thought

There is an intriguing sentence in the part of René Cassin's memoirs where he describes the efforts of the Human Rights Commission to secure support from as many nations as possible when the Declaration was presented for adoption by the U.N. General Assembly at its Paris session in the fall of 1948. According to Cassin, the commission was aided on several occasions by the "discreet personal encouragements" of the papal nuncio in Paris, one Angelo Roncalli.[12] The future John XXIII must have agreed with Maritain and other Catholic thinkers that there was value in discussing certain human goods as rights, even though the language of rights could never be the mother tongue of Christians. For when he became pope, he described the UDHR as "an act of the highest importance."[13]

Many Catholics were surprised, and some were even shocked, at the extent to which the documents of Vatican II and John XXIII's encyclicals *Pacem in Terris* and *Mater et Magistra* seemed to effect a shift from natural law to human rights. I agree with those who regard this shift as more rhetorical than theoretical, an effort on the part of the church to make her own teachings intelligible to "all men and women of good will."[14] But with that shift came significant risks and the need to be very clear about the fact that the church did not always use terminology in the same way it was used in secular circles. Passages like the following from *Pacem in Terris*, for example, may sound like the Universal Declaration, but are grounded in Christian anthropology and conditioned by Christian understandings of what rights are *for*:

> Beginning our discussion of the rights of man, we see that every man has the right to life, to bodily integrity, and to the means which are necessary and suitable for the proper development of life; these are primarily food, clothing, shelter, rest, medical care, and finally the necessary social services. Therefore a human being also has the right

to security in cases of sickness, inability to work, widowhood, old age, unemployment, or in any other case in which he is deprived of the means of subsistence through no fault of his own [11].

Vatican II, we now know, only marked the beginning of the church's appropriation of modern rights talk. One of the council fathers, Karol Wojtyla of Krakow, would travel even further along that road when he became John Paul II.[15] He has often praised the Universal Declaration of Human Rights, calling it "a real milestone on the path of the moral progress of humanity," and "one of the highest expressions of the human conscience of our time."[16] As Avery Dulles has written, "Of all the popes in history, none has given so much emphasis to human rights as John Paul II."[17]

Critics of these developments have rightly noted their risks, but they have often failed to notice four important facts about the church's use of rights language. First, the rights tradition into which the church has tapped is the dignitarian tradition which she herself had already done so much to shape, not the highly individualistic, libertarian tradition which Anglo-Americans often take as the only or the best way of thinking about rights. "The Catholic doctrine of human rights," Father Dulles points out, "is not based on Lockean empiricism or individualism. It has a more ancient and distinguished pedigree."[18]

Second, in no sense did the church uncritically adopt even the dignitarian vision as her own. Already in *Gaudium et Spes*, the council fathers warned that the movement to respect human rights "must be imbued with the spirit of the Gospel and be protected from all appearance of mistaken autonomy. We are tempted to consider our personal rights as fully protected only when we are free from every norm of divine law; but following this road leads to the destruction rather than to the maintenance of the dignity of the human person."[19] Similarly, in *Pacem in Terris*, John XXIII noted that "Some objections and reservations . . . were raised regarding certain points in the declaration, and rightly so" (144). Everything the church says about human rights is conditioned by their foundation in the dignity that attaches to the person made in the image and likeness of God, and everything is oriented to the end of the common good, defined in *Gaudium et Spes* as "the sum of those conditions of social life by which individuals, families and groups can achieve their own fulfillment in a relatively thorough and ready way" (74).

Third, the new terminology of rights is closely connected to traditional teachings concerning obligations. The church is concerned as much about the souls of those who disregard the dignity of others as she is for those to whom obligations are owed.

And finally, the most distinctive feature of the church's posture toward the modern human rights project has been encouragement, accompanied by constructive but pointed criticism. Thus, for example, when John Paul II sent his good wishes on the occasion of the fiftieth birthday of the Declaration, he warned that "Certain shadows hover over the anniversary, consisting in the reservations being expressed in relation to two essential characteristics of the very idea of human rights: their *universality* and their *indivisibility*."[20]

3. Potential Contributions of Catholic Learning to the Dilemmas of Universality, Indivisibility, Foundations, and Truth

The fact is that "certain shadows" have hovered over the universal rights idea from the beginning. Can any rights really be said to be universal in a constantly changing world composed of many different cultures? Can freedom really coexist with a broad array of rights to social security? What is the basis for human rights? Is belief in human rights just a leap of faith? In the remainder of this essay, I suggest some ways in which Catholic thinkers could be especially helpful with four persistent dilemmas facing the human rights project—particularly if they can deepen, develop, and communicate the wisdom the church has gleaned through the ages concerning inculturation, solidarity, subsidiarity, and the ability of the properly formed human mind to progress toward knowledge of objective truth.

Universal Rights in Diverse Cultures

Let us begin with the challenge posed to universality by cultural diversity. The claim that every human being is entitled to certain basic rights simply by virtue of being human has come under increasing attack from a variety of directions. To take one prominent example, the standard response of China's leaders, when criticized for rights violations, is that all rights are relative. A number of Islamic governments, and leaders of some developing countries, have taken the position that some so-called universal rights are just masks for cultural imperialism aimed at imposing "Western" or "Judeo-Christian" ideas on the rest of the world. Meanwhile, in the West, it has become fashionable to deny that there is any such thing as a universally valid proposition about human beings or human affairs. None of these challenges can be lightly dismissed. Certainly it is no answer to simply assert, as does the U.N.'s 1993 Vienna Human Rights Declaration, that the universality of these rights is "beyond question."[21]

The long Catholic experience in the dialectic between universal principles and diverse cultures provides encouraging evidence, though, that universality need not entail homogeneity, and that pluralism does not necessarily entail relativism. The history of inculturation of the Christian faith in many different societies also shows that the common understanding of core truths can be enriched by the accumulation of a variety of experiences in living those truths.

John Paul II, in his 1995 address to the fiftieth General Assembly of the United Nations, applied that body of knowledge to the dilemma of the universality of human rights. Universal rights and particular cultures, he said, cannot be radically opposed. After all, rights emerge from culture; rights cannot be sustained without cultural underpinnings; and rights, to be effective, must become part of each people's way of life. Different cultures are "but different ways of facing the question of the meaning of personal existence."[22] Thus there can be a "legitimate pluralism" in forms of freedom, with different means of expressing and protecting basic rights, provided "that in every case the levels set for the whole of humanity by the Universal Declaration are respected."[23] As Jacques Maritain nicely put it long ago, there could be many different kinds of music played on the Declaration's thirty strings.[24]

From centuries of evangelization efforts, and from her dialogue with political philosophy, the church has absorbed another important lesson about human affairs: that personal formation is essential to cultural formation and that no program for advancing the common good is secure unless it rests on firm cultural foundations. Indeed, John Paul II sounds much like Alexis de Tocqeville when he points out that "Only when a culture of human rights which respects different traditions becomes an integral part of humanity's moral patrimony shall we be able to look to the future with serene confidence,"[25] or when he says that "the dignity of the individual must be safeguarded by custom before the law can do so."[26]

The bottom-up approach to protecting human dignity in Catholic thought corresponds perfectly with the understanding of universality shared by the principal architects of the Universal Declaration: Eleanor

Roosevelt, René Cassin, Charles Malik, and the Chinese philosopher-diplomat Peng-chun Chang. The records of their deliberations are replete with statements showing that they never intended that its common standard of achievement would or should produce completely uniform practices. One of the most pointed examples occurs in Chang's speech urging the U.N. General Assembly to adopt the declaration. The peoples of the world, he said, had had enough of the sort of uniformity that colonial powers once sought to impose on them—a standardized way of thinking and a single way of life. That sort of uniformity could only be achieved by force or at the expense of truth. It could never last.

By contrast, today's human rights activists, influenced more than they realize by American legal ideas that came into vogue in the 1960s, tend almost instinctively to think in terms of legalistic, top-down solutions, and to forget about the primacy of culture. The numbers of international lawyers who recall the wisdom of the framers are diminishing. One such, however, is Philip Alston, who wrote on the UDHR's thirty-fifth anniversary that "The Declaration does not purport to offer a single unified conception of the world as it should be nor does it purport to offer some sort of comprehensive recipe for the attainment of an ideal world. Its purpose is rather the more modest one of proclaiming a set of values which are capable of giving some guidance to modern society in choosing among a wide range of alternative policy options."[27]

Indivisibility

I hope I have said enough to indicate some ways in which Catholic experience might be helpful to the dilemma of reconciling universality of human rights with cultural diversity. A second dilemma arises from the perennial tension between certain rights, for example, between freedom and social security. The 1948 Declaration, like the Catholic social doctrine which influenced it in this respect, insists on the mutual dependence between political and civil rights on the one hand, and social justice on the other. The rights it contains are said to be indivisible.

No sooner was the ink dry on the UDHR, however, than the Cold War antagonists put asunder what the framers had joined together. The Eisenhower State Department dismissed the social and economic provisions as "socialistic," while their Soviet counterparts derided the traditional eighteenth-century rights as "bourgeois."

What began as expediency hardened into habit. Today, the Declaration is almost universally approached by friend and foe alike as Americans approach the Bill of Rights, that is, as a kind of menu from which one can pick and choose according to one's taste. The more affluent countries (and even the major human rights organizations which are based in such countries) concern themselves hardly at all with the articles relating to social and economic justice. Meanwhile, leaders of some developing countries ignore political and civil liberties in favor of social and economic rights, or insist that human rights are luxuries which need to be put on hold for the sake of national security or economic development. Without devaluing the good work the international human rights movement has done for victims of torture and discrimination, it must also be said that this case-and-controversy–oriented movement has nearly lost sight of the fact that the Universal Declaration embodies a wider, integrated conception of rights. The movement itself needs to be reminded of the fact that "when the violation of any fundamental human right is accepted without reaction, all other rights are placed at risk.[28] One of the most pressing challenges for friends of the universal human rights idea, therefore, is to reunite the two halves of the divided soul of the Declaration—its commitment to human liberty and its acknowledgment of a single human family for which all bear a common responsibility.

In a development that few would have anticipated fifty years ago, the Catholic Church has become the principal institutional defender in the world today of the Universal Declaration as an integrated whole. There is no way to exaggerate the importance of the presence of the Holy See in the U.N. in keeping alive the connection between freedom and solidarity—at a time when affluent nations seem increasingly to be washing their hands of poor countries and peoples. Time and again, John Paul II has challenged those who would emphasize individual liberty but neglect social justice. In his speech to the U.N. on its fiftieth anniversary, for example, he said: "Inspired by the example of all those who have taken the *risk of freedom*, can we not recommit ourselves also to taking the *risk of solidarity*— and thus the *risk of peace*?"[29] The pleas of this pope on behalf of social justice go largely unreported, yet they are at least as deeply challenging and far more "judgmental" than anything this pope has ever said about human sexuality. Consider, for example:

> The distinctive mark of the Christian, today more than ever, must be love for the poor, the weak, the suffering. Living out this demanding

commitment requires a total reversal of the alleged values which make people seek only their own good: power, pleasure, the unscrupulous accumulation of wealth. . . . A society of genuine solidarity can be built only if the well-off in helping the poor, do not stop at giving from what they do not need. . . . Those living in poverty can wait no longer: They need help now and so have a right to receive immediately what they need.[30]

Strongly worded as are these calls to solidarity from the pen of John Paul II, they are mild in comparison to what Jacques Maritain wrote in the UNESCO philosophers' volume on human rights:

It is an irony stained with blood to think that . . . the atheist ideology [of socialism] is a heritage from the most "bourgeois" representatives of the bourgeoisie, who, after calling on the god of the Deists that they might base their own demands on the natural law, rejected that God and the God of the Christians alike when they were come to power and sought to free the all-embracing exercise of proprietary rights from the shackles of the natural law, and to close their ears to the cry of the poor.[31]

Again, it is important to note that much confusion exists about the relation of Catholic social thought to similar-sounding secular ideas. The church teaches solidarity as a virtue which relates to the perfection of the individual,[32] by inclining us to overcome sources of division within ourselves (personal sin) and within society ("astructural sins").[33] The virtue of solidarity is thus inseparable from personal reform and requires constant practice. It can hardly be equated with crude mandates for state-directed programs for redistributing wealth or restructuring institutions, nor with the kind of solidarity that exalts the group over the individual. But it is highly compatible with the intent of UDHR framers like Chang, who maintained that the principal goal of the Declaration should be "to build up better human beings," and Charles Malik, who wrote that "Men, cultures and nations must first mature inwardly" before human rights can be a reality.

With regard to the formidable problem of how to move from the principle of solidarity to its practical implementation under diverse social and political conditions, the church of course has no specific models to propose.[34] In this area where the state of human knowledge is not far advanced, and practically everything remains to be done, she does, however, have several potentially fruitful insights. Her principle of subsidiarity, for example, is already implicit in the Universal Declaration, as is her understanding that freedom and justice have conditions. Though subsidiarity is attracting increasing attention from political thinkers, it is an idea that needs to be deepened and developed.[35] And what would be more fitting than that Catholic thinkers should take the initiative in clarifying and developing this potentially useful concept?

That, of course, would require Catholic thinkers to become familiar with their own social tradition, in emulation of Charles Malik.[36] In this connection, it seems appropriate to mention the recent lament of the American bishops that "our social doctrine is not shared or taught in a consistent and comprehensive way in too many of our schools, seminaries, religious education programs, colleges and universities."[37]

Catholics would also have to come to terms with the sad fact that, just as "certain shadows" have fallen over the UDHR's link between freedom and social justice, so a shadow has fallen over the connection between Catholic social thought and the moral teachings that undergird it. All too many Catholics seem to want the preferential option for the poor without attending to the habits and conditions that make such a commitment sustainable. All too many others seem to resist the teaching that living the whole Christian faith means living the option for the poor.

The Dilemma of Foundations

A third area where Catholic thinkers might benefit the human rights project concerns some business that the drafters of the Universal Declaration left unfinished—namely, the problem of supplying firm foundations for the practical consensus they had achieved on human rights. The framers of the Declaration forged ahead, under pressure of time, on the basis of that consensus. The surprisingly similar lists of fundamental principles the UNESCO philosophers and the U.N. Human Rights Division discovered in their cross-national surveys gave them confidence that foundations could be supplied, but they had to leave the demonstration for another day. It had been easy for representatives of different religions and cultures to agree on the rights, Jacques Maritain famously said, so long as no one asked why.[38]

Today, however, the problem of foundations has acquired new urgency. The close of the Cold War has seen a surge of bloody regional and ethnic conflicts that have impaired the sense of the unity of the human family. Economic and technological developments have brought new risks that human beings will be treated as instruments or objects. Fashionable philosophies deny the existence of truth or the ability of the human mind to grasp it. As Dulles points out, "Without a sound basis in philosophical anthropology, the human rights tradition can be easily dismissed or perverted."[39]

The shallowness of much contemporary thinking about the foundations of human rights is exemplified by Michael Ignatieff's recent article in the *New York Review of Books*.[40] Posing the question of why we should "believe that human beings should not be beaten, tortured, coerced, indoctrinated, or in any way sacrificed against their will," Ignatieff replies that this ethic "derives from our own experience of pain and our capacity to imagine the pain of others." Apparently unaware that he has reproduced almost word for word Rousseau's argument for compassion as the basis of morality, Ignatieff also fails to realize that the shakiness of that foundation has long since been exposed. Empathy is just a feeling, and a transient one at that. It yields easily, as Rousseau himself conceded, to self-preservation and, one might add, to self-interest.[41] Something sturdier is needed to engender the habits that impel people to respect the dignity of others—and to set the conditions under which human rights will be respected.

The time thus seems overdue to provide the universal rights idea with a more secure philosophical basis.[42] Václav Havel seems to have had some such project in mind when he proposed on the Declaration's fiftieth anniversary that the United Nations undertake "a quest for a common denominator of spiritual values uniting the different cultures of our present world."[43] The UNESCO philosophers' committee long ago realized, however, that the quest for a single foundation of human rights would almost certainly prove fruitless. They concluded that "the members of the United Nations share common convictions upon which human rights depend, but . . . that those common convictions are stated in terms of different philosophic principles and on the background of divergent political and economic systems."[44]

As Ralph McInerny has explained, Maritain and his colleagues were proceeding on the assumptions that common appreciations of the human good are embedded in diverse traditions, and that they can be formulated abstractly in such a way as to enable all concerned to stand on principle, even though the principles on which they stand are different.[45] That line of thinking seems similar to what John Paul II had in mind when he told the Vatican diplomatic corps in 1989 that it is now the task of "the various schools of thought—especially communities of believers—to tackle the job of furnishing the legal framework governing the rights of mankind with a moral foundation" (7).

At last, after fifty years, those assumptions are being tested. Serious investigations are taking place into the ways in which the world's cultural, philosophical, and religious traditions have affirmed the unity of the human family and the universality of certain basic human goods that have been cast in modern times as fundamental rights.[46]

As Catholic scholars join in that endeavor, no doubt they will find their own thinking about human dignity deepened and enriched in the process. Christians, we are told in *Centesimus Annus*, are obliged not only to bring light to the world, but also to remain open to discover "every fragment of truth . . . in the life experience and in the culture of individuals and nations" (46). As Alasdair MacIntyre has reminded us, a living tradition is distinguished not only by its continuity, but by its dynamism.[47] And, I would add, a great tradition is distinguished not only by what it can contribute to the world's stock of wisdom, but by its ability to borrow judiciously from other stores.

It will be good news if, as the framers and UNESCO philosophers predicted, the Declaration's principles can be shown to be deeply rooted in the world's major philosophical and religious traditions and thus in the shared history of the human race. Documenting that proposition would improve the chances for a truly universal dialogue about how we are to order our lives together on this conflict-ridden, but interdependent planet. But sooner rather than later, any such dialogue will have to confront the challenges of historicism and relativism.

The Dilemma of Truth

If there are no common truths to which all men and women can appeal, then there are no human rights, and there is little hope that reason and choice can prevail over force and accident in the realm of human affairs.[48] It is one thing to acknowledge, with St. Paul, that the human mind can glimpse truth only as through a glass darkly (1 Corinthians 13:12), and quite another to deny the existence of truth altogether. Hannah Arendt has warned of the grave practical implications of everyday nihilism, arguing persuasively that "the ideal subject of totalitarian rule is not the convinced

Nazi or the convinced communist, but people for whom the distinction between fact and fiction (i.e., the reality of experience) and the distinction between true and false (i.e., the standards of thought) no longer exist."[49] John Paul II puts it this way: "[T]he root of modern totalitarianism is to be found in the denial of the transcendent dignity of the human person."[50]

But we postmoderns must ask—how do we know what is true? Here, again, is an area where practically everything remains to be done. I would only point out that, in the world today, where relativism and historicism rule the secular academy, the Catholic Church, again to the surprise of many, has stepped forward as an unabashed defender of reason, notably with the remarkable encyclical *Fides et Ratio*. Hers is not the calculating reason of Hobbes in the service of the passions, nor the narrow scientific rationalism of the French *lumières*, but rather the dynamic, recurrent, and potentially self-correcting processes of human knowing.

It does not seem too much to hope that this may be the moment for Catholic universities to be true to their highest calling by preserving the dynamic interaction between tradition and the spirit of free inquiry that is not, alas, enjoying its finest hour in secular American universities. The time is ripe, I believe, to ponder carefully the work of religious thinkers like the Jesuit philosopher Bernard Lonergan, who takes modern historical consciousness and the diversity of cultures seriously, but who finds the basis for objectivity in "the dynamic unity of the human mind in its related and recurrent operations."[51]

I trust that my confidence in the unexplored potential of Catholic intellectual traditions will not be understood as unbridled Catholic triumphalism. As John Paul II himself reminds us, the church approaches the third millennium "on her knees," painfully aware of the ways in which her sons and daughters through history have fallen short in thought, word, and deed. Much of what her intellectual tradition has to offer was learned painfully after mistakes and sad experiences.

There is, however, such a thing as exaggerated self-criticism. At a time and in a culture where religion, reason, and human rights alike are under siege from so many directions, I believe those of us who are teachers do a great disservice if by our words or our silence we contribute to the myth that the history of Christianity in general and Catholicism in particular is a history of patriarchy, worldliness, or exclusion of people or ideas. We have inherited a great tradition of free inquiry and fearless engagement with ideas. We should rejoice in that tradition—and resolve to use it.

NOTES

1. No one has done more to acquaint the Anglo-American legal world with the existence and meaning of the dignitarian rights tradition than Donald Kommers; see his description of the dignity-based German Basic Law in *The Constitutional Jurisprudence of the Federal Republic of Germany*, 2d ed. (Durham, N.C.: Duke University Press, 1997), 30–40.

2. For a discussion of Catholic influences on the Universal Declaration in general, Philippe de la Chappelle, *La Déclaration universelle des droits de l'homme et le Catholicisme* (Paris: Librairie Générale de Droit et de Jurisprudence, 1967).

3. U.N. UDHR, arts. 22–25.

4. Ibid., preamble and arts. 1, 16, 22, 25, and 26.

5. Unless otherwise specified, the references to the history of the Universal Declaration are from Mary Ann Glendon, *Rights from Wrongs* (forthcoming, Random House).

6. See Mary Ann Glendon, *Rights Talk: The Impoverishment of Political Discourse* (New York: Free Press, 1991).

7. *Populorum Progressio*, 13.

8. Johannes Morsink, *The Universal Declaration of Human Rights: Origins, Drafting, and Intent* (Philadelphia: University of Pennsylvania Press, 1999), 1.

9. Avery Dulles, *Human Rights: The United Nations and Papal Teaching* (New York: Fordham University Press, 1999), 4.

10. John P. Humphrey, *Human Rights and the United Nations: A Great Adventure* (Dobbs Ferry, N.Y.: Transnational Publishing, 1984), 65–66.

11. *On the Edge of Greatness: The Diaries of John Humphrey*, ed. A. J. Hobbins, 3 vols. (Montreal: McGill University Libraries, 1994), 1:87.

12. René Cassin, "Vatican II et la Protection de la Personne," *Journal des Communautés* 13 (1966): 17.

13. *Pacem in Terris*, 143.

14. John Finnis, *Natural Law and Natural Rights* (New York: Oxford University Press, 1980).

15. See Giorgio Filibeck, "Human Rights in the Teachings of John Paul II: Bases and Principles," *Al Abhath: Journal of the Faculty of Arts and Sciences, American University of Beirut* 46 (1998): 29; *Human Rights in the Teaching of the Church: From John XXIII to John Paul II* (Vatican City: Libreria Editrice Vaticana, 1994).

16. "Address to the United Nations" (2 October 1979), 7; "Address to the United Nations" (5 October 1995), 2.

17. Dulles, *Human Rights*, 5.

18. Ibid., 12.

19. *Gaudium et Spes*, 41.

20. "World Day of Peace Message, 1998," 2.

21. World Conference on Human Rights (A/CONF.157/24), Vienna Declaration and Program of Action, I, art. 5.

22. "Address to the United Nations" (5 October 1995), 9.

23. "World Day of Peace Message, 1999," 3.

24. Jacques Maritain, *Man and the State* (Chicago: University of Chicago Press, 1951), 106.

25. "World Day of Peace Message, 1999," 12.

26. "Address to the Diplomatic Corps, 1989," 7.

27. Philip Alston, "The Universal Declaration at 35: Western and Passé or Alive and Universal," *International Commission of Jurists Review* 30 (1983): 60–61.

28. "World Day of Peace Message, 1999," 12.

29. "Address to the United Nations" (5 October 1995), 15.

30. "World Day of Peace Message, 1997," 8.

31. Jacques Maritain, "On the Philosophy of Human Rights," in *Human Rights: Comments and Interpretations* (New York: Columbia University Press, 1949), 72, 76.

32. See Ernest Fortin, "Church Activism in the 1980s," in *Collected Essays*, ed. Brian Benestad, vol. 3 (Lanham, Md.: Rowman and Littlefield, 1996), 261, 273–74; Brian Benestad, "What Do Catholics Know about Catholic Social Thought?" in *Festschrift for George Kelly* (forthcoming Christendom Press).

33. *Solicitudo Rei Socialis,* 37, 38.

34. See *Populorum Progressio,* 13, 81; *Solicitudo Rei Socialis,* 41.

35. See Peter Berger and Richard J. Neuhaus, *To Empower People: From State to Civil Society,* 2d ed. (Washington, D.C.: American Enterprise Institute, 1996); George Liebmann, *The Little Platoons: Sub-Local Governments in Modern History* (London: Praeger, 1995), and *The Gallows in the Grove: Civil Society in American Law* (London: Praeger, 1997).

36. Benestad, "What Do Catholics Know?"

37. U.S. Catholic Bishops, *Sharing Catholic Social Teaching* (Washington, D.C.: U.S.C.C., 1998), 3.

38. Maritain, Introduction, in *Human Rights,* 9.

39. Dulles, *Human Rights,* 17.

40. Michael Ignatieff, "Human Rights: The Mid-Life Crisis," *New York Review of Books,* 20 May 1999, 58.

41. Jean-Jacques Rousseau, *Discourse on the Origin of Inequality*, in *The Social Contract and Discourses*, trans. G. D. H. Cole (New York: Dutton, 1973), 42.

42. In his "Address to the Diplomatic Corps, 1989" John Paul II speaks of the need "to tackle the job of furnishing the legal framework governing the rights of mankind with a moral foundation," and suggests that "the Catholic Church—and perhaps other spiritual families—has a unique contribution to make." (7)

43. "Havel's Speech on 50th Anniversary of Human Rights Declaration," Czech News Agency, March 16, 1998.

44. UNESCO Committee on the Theoretical Bases of Human Rights, Final Report, in Dulles, *Human Rights,* 258–59.

45. Ralph McInerny, "Natural Law and Human Rights," *American Journal of Jurisprudence* 36 (1991): 1, 14.

46. See "On Human Rights: Declaration of Human Rights Fifty Years Later, A Statement of the Ramsey Colloquium," *First Things,* April 1998, 18.

47. Alasdair MacIntyre, *After Virtue* (Notre Dame, Ind.: University of Notre Dame Press, 1981), 206–7.

48. "If there is no transcendent truth, in obedience to which man achieves his full identity, then there is no sure principle for guaranteeing just relations between people," *Centesimus Annus,* 29.

49. Hannah Arendt, *The Origins of Totalitarianism*, 2d ed. (New York: Meridian Books, 1958), 474.

50. *Centesimus Annus*, 44.

51. Matthew L. Lamb, "Divine Transcendence and Eternity: The Early Lonergan's Recovery of Thomas Aquinas as a Response to Father McCool's Question," in *Continuity and Plurality in Catholic Theology: Essays in Honor of Gerald A. McCool, S.J.*, ed. Anthony J. Cernera (Fairfield, Conn.: Sacred Heart University Press, 1998), 75–76.

7

What Have We Learned?

JEAN BETHKE ELSHTAIN

TO THE MOST ARDENT AND POORLY INFORMED "SECULARIST,"[1] religion and higher learning are incompatibles. I refer to those who view faith as a lunge toward inarticulate belief, hence a commitment of the sort that precludes rational, complex, nuanced interpretation and argument. Faith, under this construal, is the naive affirmation of truths the believer knows to be true because "the Bible tells me so." To the secularist, this is not only childlike, it is *childish* and constitutes *prima facie* evidence that the believer is stuck in a pre-Enlightenment miasma and, worst of all, wishes to throw this shroud of ignorance over everybody else. So committed are those I am calling ardent secularists to a version of the fundamental irrationality and atavistic nature of faith—aided and abetted, it must be said, by radically fideistic and literalist forms of Christian belief— that, at one point not so long ago, they could and did predict confidently the historic phasing out of all such forms of ignorance.

I remember well attending a lecture on a university campus—it was 1964 or thereabouts—and the lecturer, a distinguished sprout of the Family Tree Huxley (Sir Julian Huxley by name) predicted with the sort of carefree self-assurance British academic aristocrats could muster forty years ago, that by the year 2000 all manner of horrors now visited upon us would have gone the way of the ancient dinosaurs: they would be blessedly extinct. And what were these horrors? There was a trio of terribles to Sir Julian's way of thinking: religion, nationalism, and one other "ism" I have now forgotten, but it was something to do with suspicion of science and technology. And *primus inter pares* among these terribles was religion. I recall being flabbergasted on that occasion that anyone, whatever his or her perspective, could be so certain of anything in the future. As it turns out, Sir Julian's is what is known as a failed prediction.

Why and how so? The distinguished essays in this volume afford a broad and dazzling panorama of answers. Let's begin with the most obvious, namely, that religion in its Catholic form and the higher learning have walked together hand in hand for several millennia. To be sure, just as there are problems with what is to be rendered to Christ and to Caesar, there are contentious and deep issues involved in responding at any point in Christian history to Tertullian's *cri de coeur*: "What has Athens to do with Jerusalem?" The general response within the learned Christian community was that Christians should "spoil the Egyptians" by appropriating from the glories of the antique world those traditions and techniques that would best serve the new Christian dispensation. This could, and sometimes did, turn into a rather instrumental attitude toward the great traditions of ancient art and philosophy—we'll keep what's helpful and toss overboard the rest. But the remarkable thing is that it was the early church that preserved ancient philosophy and art and criticism when these might so easily have perished in the convulsions that swept over the late antique–early medieval world and that have come to be known to us, misleadingly, as "the Fall of the Roman Empire" and the "early Dark Ages." All those copyists laboring in poorly lit, cold scriptoria preserving all those texts: it is in many ways a stirring story.

I don't want to romanticize or sweep under the carpet (or the tapestry, as the case may be) the many issues that vexed Christian thinkers from then till now. I do want to dispel any notion that Christians were, to the man and woman, pious if not fanatic believers who desired to overturn all that had gone before. As well, I want to challenge the prototypical and stereotypical image of the believer as an anti-intellectual under the sway of fideistic mind control. One might call this the "Jesse Ventura" maneuver. Jesse Ventura, for foreign readers, is the ex-professional wrestler, "Reform Party" libertarian who is currently serving as governor of Minnesota and who recently delivered himself up of the old canard that believers are "weak" people who need a "crutch" and, by weak, he meant in every respect people who can't, like libertarian professional wrestlers, stand on their own two feet and use their own brains. It is also the view represented in such popular cinematic dramas as *Inherit the Wind*, a play and celebrated film about the so-called Scopes Monkey Trial in Tennessee in the 1920s. The case was a rather complicated matter, scarcely the cut-and-dried farce cum morality play in which wise, liberal, freethinkers go nose-to-nose to fend off the threat represented by ignorant Tennessee fundamentalists, bumpkins one and all, or so the film suggests.[2] Almost every red-blooded American child goes through a phase—I certainly did—of looking down on silly believers, especially one's parents. One wises up over time as one realizes the extraordinary complexities of the engagement of faith and reason, of learning and belief.[3] But *Inherit the Wind* and dozens of other films like it represent believers in a mode that makes them perfect foils for humor pitched at about the level of a typical fifteen-year-old.

Let me note yet another complexity before turning to what we have learned from reading the challenging contributions in this volume that address directly the ways in which Catholicism and the higher learning are intertwined. I have in mind the Protestant-Catholic distinction. There are so many strands of Protestantism one can fall into dangerous generalities, so let me be specific by being somewhat autobiographical. I was raised in a Lutheran tradition that has always been of several minds on the higher learning. One reads Martin Luther with occasional gasps on this very question. Luther, a learned man who thought and wrote with extraordinary power, could nonetheless deliver himself up of views that seem hostile to philosophic speculation in any mode but most pointedly in the Scholastic form that prevailed in the universities of his own time. Luther, typically, always uses a nuclear weapon when a mere howitzer might do, so he sets about pulverizing Aristotle's *Ethics*, among other works that to him represent an idle or possibly perverse use of the mind.

These moments in Luther certainly lend credence to charges that Christians are anti-philosophical, if not anti-intellectual. At the same time, Lutheran Christians, like Catholics, were devoted to education. Christian formation was central to each tradition and, in the United States, Lutherans created their own colleges to press forward with higher learning in the service of faith and faith in the service of higher learning. Throughout, however, there lurked the suspicion that wedding theology too tightly to philosophy was a temptation to error. The Catholic tradition, by contrast, did not advance in the same way strands of outright hostility to some forms of higher learning, having, for example, come to grips with the issue of evolution well before so many of their Protestant brothers and sisters. Why? In part, surely, because of the long lifting up of "scientific reason" as a legitimate, at times even glorious, use of the intellect.[4] So, before the caveats and prefaces grow even longer, let's turn to the uses of the intellect through the prism of "Higher Learning and Catholic Traditions."

What resources has Catholic thought to bring to bear? Alive in the higher learning in divinity schools these days is a word derived from biblical scholarship, namely, *ressourcement*, a bringing to bear of the resources a tradition offers as a way of releasing the vibrancy of that tradition. *Ressourcement* is not a slogan covering up hard-core traditionalism; rather, it is a rich word for a rich phenomenon and imperative, one that is poised in tandem with *aggiornamento*, or opening the windows to new currents, rather than in opposition to such fresh breezes. This by no means suggests smooth sailing as one considers visions of learning in relation to the church. There are many sources of irritation and affirmation, whether one is prelate or scholar, citizen of the pew or denizen of the archive. What the Erasmus Institute at the University of Notre Dame aims to do is to reaffirm a sturdy connection between Catholicism and the higher learning. The proof in such matters is always in the pudding—in works of scholarship that display the fruitfulness of the connection between the Abrahamic intellectual traditions in general and those of Catholicism in particular. There are both possibilities and perils whenever one embarks on such an enterprise. Many complex matters need to be unpacked.

The first unpacker, the distinguished philosopher Alasdair MacIntyre, sets the tone for this volume in emphasizing the vital need for an *integrative approach to higher learning*. What does he have in mind? And how is this integrative imperative to be pursued and to be met?

I will flesh out a focus on the human person as the nodal point and grounding for such an overall integrative task as we go along. Let's concentrate, first, on MacIntyre's argument as it pertains to the contemporary university. For MacIntyre, it is exigent that a Catholic university understand its integrative task better and that it bring to bear the many intellectual resources of the Catholic tradition in doing so. Integration is undertaken not so much as part of a quest for the holy grail of unbending certainty but, rather, as a sustained effort in service to the perplexity that haunts the educated mind. The educated mind must be one capable of astonishment, MacIntyre insists. What should astonish us daily is that there is a magnificent, intricate order of things that makes possible our knowledge and, at the same time, places constraints on our knowing: we cannot plumb the depths entirely. But we can, if our education has been sufficiently integrative, put questions of human flourishing or failing—in relation to our complex, many-layered order of things—that those immersed in various functionalist or reductive utilitarianisms can neither put nor make sense of.

Once upon a time the theological standpoint was the integrator *par excellence* as the "queen of the sciences." Theology, long ago dethroned in favor of something called rationalism or the scientific method or nothing at all, became, instead, a poor stepsister within the academy, to the extent she was permitted entry at all. Theology was what "they" did at seminaries and in academic eddies and backwaters. MacIntyre offers a rationale for turning this situation upside down. In our time we desperately require what we have lost, namely, a point of view that helps us make sense of many points of view. Perhaps a philosophical theology up to this daunting task can be restored to the place it once occupied, though, of course, it will occupy that place very differently, having been challenged and shaped by all the strong breezes and currents of the last eight centuries or more. On MacIntyre's view, a comprehensive neo-Thomism affords just such a stirring and complex mode of rational inquiry. Of course, this enterprise needs justification. No truth is simply "self-evident," pace America's founding fathers.

A brief reminder is in order. The university's inception lies in the idea of *universitas*, something encompassing. Our modern universities, seeing no need for such a mission, have largely abandoned the encompassing for the highly specialized that eschews an integrative task: all is fission and fragment. Keenly aware of what he sees as a deeply debilitating phenomenon, MacIntyre offers two rival conceptions of the university, not unlike his treatment of rival conceptions of moral inquiry. But the choice before us here is not Aristotle v. Nietzsche but, rather, *random* pluralism v. integration. The latter, in complex ways, is accountable to the church and the church's faithfulness to her mission; the former is not.[5] For MacIntyre, this cashes out as an urgent plea for neo-Aristotelian Thomism, and although integration is much in the air in this volume, no other candidates for prime integrator on the level of a thinker or system of thought were proffered. Absent integration, argued MacIntyre, we are stuck with a random collection of experts.[6] Integration is a challenging task that requires a real, sustained effort. Randomness requires no explicit effort since it will happen more or less automatically, given the drift that is coded into the interstices of the modern research university.

All participants in the higher learning carry the seeds of randomness about with them and sow them with abandon. Students have been taught that they need and even have a "right" to demand an education that is guaranteed to be "relevant" and will get them a fast-track career and a ticket into a higher tax bracket. But an authentically liberal education cannot be either narrowly specialized or simply vocational. Higher learning at home under the big tent of robust integration will, among other things, help to liberate the minds of students from these and other preconceptions of the wider culture about what education is for. Over the years, partial liberation from the excessively materialistic and individualistic demands of the wider culture as a feature of scholarly formation has been a Catholic aim. When education is reduced to narrowly instrumental career-planning, young people are forced to make many of the key choices of their lives prematurely: they are treated more like consumers than like apprentice learners. Life becomes a compartmentalized series of jerks and starts in which students learn to play *roles* under the aegis of utilitarian and emotivist imperatives. But the student who is formed within an integrative context can, if all has gone well, stand back and assess the standards of human flourishing she has absorbed. Integration offers notions of a plurality of goods as well as ways to evaluate these goods—all in the knowledge that learning must partake in vital ways in the ancient and noble ideal of *vita contemplativa*.

At stake is the *formation of character* in and through a form of integrated understanding that is possible (if conspicuous by its absence nowadays) in higher learning. This often means resisting institutional inertia of a very pressing type, but faculty alone can begin the process of reforming graduate schools and finding ways to involve undergraduates in integrative projects. Only in this way, MacIntyre concludes, can the random colonization of plural (but related) scholarly enterprises be forestalled.

What does this mean? I take it to mean the happenstance but nonetheless thorough manner in which ancillary disciplines can be readily "colonized" by an energetic model or method vying to be "queen [more likely king] of the sciences," as, for example, rational choice theory does currently. A mathematically elegant microeconomic theory undergirds the preoccupation with rational choice. But the result, at least for normative inquiry with an ethical intent, is that the rational-choice econometric imperative has squeezed out space for normative inquiry with an ethical intent in political science, sociology, and chunks of history. Those not given over to rational choice theory may drift in another direction, say, toward poststructuralist literary theory. These aggressive bear hugs from the econometric and high-flying "lit-crit" directions, respectively, have happened willy-nilly rather than as part of a worked-out strategy of integration. And they have had the effect of narrowing modes of inquiry and making them more formulaic. The upshot is a form of inertia brought about by randomness, and this makes projects of integration dauntingly difficult, if not impossible, at least on the dominant view. That view holds that in an era of radical pluralization, it is not feasible to embrace an integrative imperative, and those who aim to do so are marginalized as hidebound traditionalists out to stymie free inquiry.

And so it comes to pass that matters get stalled and continue to sputter along willy-nilly. To be sure, MacIntyre's candidate for integration—neo-Thomism—is controversial. But that is precisely what we will be debating once integration is on the agenda. Every living tradition, MacIntyre insists, is a continuing debate. What is at stake in all this is the shape and purpose of people's lives. That issue suggests a question: Does going to graduate school make you a better or a worse person? Alas, too often these days, one comes out worse rather than better, with one's moral compass and reasoning capacities skewed in a purely instrumental direction.

Let's turn to sociology, a field which, if learned, would make you a better person today, at least on MacIntyre's view. How so? Alan Wolfe's survey of the current sociological scene as a case study of the best and the worst of higher learning in our late-modern context helps to explain. For Wolfe, sociology as a discipline and Catholicism as a tradition share a good deal, beginning with the fact that each is an enterprise that claims it is the bearer of a truth, or of truths to which the world should pay attention. But matters drift apart rather radically after that, beginning with sociology's self-understanding. The great founders of sociology—Emile Durkheim and Max Weber among them—embraced sociology as a "secular religion," a substitute for a previously faith-based comprehensive worldview. Durkheim was a fervent proponent of a kind of organicist civil religion in the service of welding citizens to *la patrie*. Weber's sociology, a by-product of the German Kulturkampf against the Catholic Church under Bismarck, insisted upon an "elective affinity" between Protestantism and sociology. Protestantism and sociology were each vehicles for modernization and for breaking individuals out of the cocoons of the past.

Unsurprisingly, sociology embraced enlightenment through empiricism. If you wanted to know "the truth," the sociologist said: go out and "measure it." The sociologist is more than an academic Sgt. Joe Friday, "Just the facts, ma'am," however, as he or she gives meaning to this empirical material. Interpretation is an unavoidable dimension of sociology. Here the "human sciences," of which sociology is one, have frequently done themselves a disservice and ill-served students and the higher learning in so doing, by driving too sharp a wedge between those truths that can be known and embraced through faith—the famous faith seeking understanding (*credo ut intelligam*) of Augustine—and truths that can be known empirically. For data never speaks for itself. Facts are not tiny homunculi with piping voices chirping out their little stories. Facts, like the truths of faith, submit to human reason in the service—ideally—of a quest for trying to get it right; trying to be as faithful as one can to "reality."

Reality has a bad press these days. For radical social constructionists, there is no such thing. Of course, everybody nowadays is a bit of a social constructionist. We know that context and historic epoch—what has gone before, what is now going on—help to determine what we know, how we come to know it, and the truth claims we make in behalf of the outcomes of our interpretive and critical projects. That said, it remains vital to launch a brief in behalf of one version or another of realism. MacIntyre, for example, voices several times the locution "critical realism." What is this, anyhow? For one thing, far too complex to present in these brief reflections. But, minimally, a commitment to realism as epistemology, interpretation, and moral imperative is a commitment to the view that we do not just fly by the seats of our pants; that the world is not just a random, happenstance thing; that there is a complex order that we can come to know, haltingly and incompletely, for that is the only way human beings can come to know. What we do over time is to deepen our engagement with reality. Perhaps sociology is in need of a return to realism, not as crude empiricism but, rather, as critical empiricism in which data gestures toward ever deeper and more complex realities about human persons, their moral standing, and the worlds of which they are a part. This, at least, is the direction one can move to get out of the conundrum in which sociology currently finds itself.

Here a great tradition of Catholic thought might be brought to bear in the service of a revivified critical sociology: Catholic social thought. Catholic social thought powerfully bridges the yawning abyss that all too often opens up between "the normative" and "the empirical" by helping us to probe what the empirical tells us about our condition normatively. With its powerful categories of *solidarity* and *subsidiarity*, Catholic social thought offers a nuanced social ecology within which we can locate the connections between things in an integrative way. The moral questions help to give energy and point to sociological inquiry, and sociological inquiry, in turn, helps to illumine how and in what ways moral questions can never be avoided or evaded. Thus, one can put together—rather than driving apart—distinctive ways of treating "the same" phenomenon. An empirical researcher, like Robert Putnam, author of the famous "bowling alone" piece cited by Wolfe, offers complex trend data on the unraveling of American civil society.[7] But this data can "speak" only if it is located within an animating vision. Here Putnam's famous essay falls somewhat short as he tacks onto the conclusion of his piece words about how the "poets" of political theory, who fretted about weakening of the interstices of democratic society, had "it" right, so we all must put our shoulders to the wheel. But we also know that there are good and bad ways to put shoulders to wheels. We would much prefer urban anomie to a robust separatist political movement based solely on racial criteria, for example. In order to assay efforts to rebuild civil society, we require an integrated vision that allows us to examine the goods of persons in community from a grounding that begins with the dignity of the human person.

Take a concrete example of how this would work using a social ecology framework derived from Catholic social thought as a conceptual frame within which to situate the facts of out-of-wedlock teen births in America, drawing together the data itself (of several varieties) and the normative implications of this phenomenon. As with the Catholic understanding of human rights, Catholic teaching and scholarship on solidarity and subsidiarity—the twin pillars of the Catholic social thought tradition—take root in the rich ground of human dignity that functions on the levels of ontology and anthropology derived from a neo-naturalist set of claims about what persons are and what persons do or are capable of doing when they are most free to be persons, that is, human beings in *communio*.

If you view the problem of out-of-wedlock teen births within this frame, you discern immediately that (a) unmarried teen-age mothering represents a break in human relationships, a tear in the fabric of community, and (b) teen-mothers and their offspring must be sustained, insofar as it is possible, within a community of love and concern that is consistent with human dignity. A way "consistent with human dignity" incorporates at its heart a critical imperative. How so? Because a breakage has already occurred and it must be "named" and mended, if possible. Within Catholic social thought, the family is the first solidaristic community the child enters, and it is basic in so many ways. The most up-to-date and best empirical social science underscores this recognition. We know that teen pregnancy is linked to drug and alcohol abuse; to high-school dropout rates that are unacceptably high; and to more teen childbearing. The babies of unwed teenage mothers are less likely to flourish than are babies born under more favorable circumstances. All too often, abuse and neglect are the companions of these children on their difficult journey, certainly in comparison with the prospects faced by children born into two-parent situations. Reported abuse for out-of-wedlock children in general is higher than for children born within a marriage, but for unwed teen mothers that rate of reported abuse is double. There are other sorts of data as well, namely, the costs to the wider society of this less-than-ideal childbearing and rearing situation. The most reliable available data tells us that teen childbearing costs some $6 billion a year to society, in direct and indirect costs. So the effects of teenage childbearing are not negligible to the well-being of the mother, the child, and the wider society. The social ecology framework tells us we must look at all the relevant facts in the situation. What it does not tell us is what is to be done.

Enter Catholic social teaching. If our social ecological framework is structured by Catholic social teaching we have some rough and ready guidelines: (1) do not do for people what they, in community, can do for themselves; (2) do not do anything to make a difficult situation worse; and (3) do everything possible to mend broken relationships and where such relationships do not exist, do everything possible to generate solidarity and sustain relationships. This suggests an interventionist stance that avoids top-down dictation but insists on the responsibility of the teenage mother herself to alter her situation. She is told: "You do not have to do this alone. We will walk with you hand in hand. But you have responsibilities, too." The social thought framework is not punitive, but it does involve forms of compulsion. There is no social world anywhere and never has been that does not involve coercion and compulsion. The question is, what form does this coercion take? What are the lines of accountability? Who is responsible for what? And so on. Immediately one dispels the watery, thinned-out notion of "Christian charity" so prevalent in the culture, including among so many Christians. It is consistent with human dignity to expect something from people, no matter how difficult their circumstance. My point for now is that the Catholic social thought framework gives us a way to interpret empirical data and to draw together what is so often driven apart through a flawed epistemology, namely, "the empirical" and, by contrast, "the normative": integration, in other words.

Starting with persons in *community*, this framework is, in many ways, *contra mundum*, for American culture is profoundly individualistic, so much so that we simply take human freestandingness as a given. Infants and children are potent signs that this is not the case and require alternative ways of thinking about human autonomy and moral freedom that recognize we are always in community, even when we deny that truth about the human condition. There is nothing we do that, in principle, is so isolated it might not touch, in some way, on another life. That is not the way we are taught to think about things. We are taught to break things into little bits and put them back together. Sometimes those bits are human beings.

But sometimes the bits are the very stuff of reality, as John Polkinghorne demonstrates in his scintillating discussion of faith and science with physics as his case in point. The connectedness of things is nowhere more evident than in modern science. Polkinghorne describes himself as a *critical realist* in his approach to the stuff of the world. I already displayed above how critical realism can be applied aptly to social science and a social problem like out-of-wedlock teen pregnancy. What does critical realism mean in general? It means taking account of all the relevant factors and features in a situation, insofar as this is humanly possible. It means trying to apprehend the truths that are there to be found and, in Polkinghorne's words, "approximated to, since even the physical science world has a richness that will always elude our total grasp." Critical realism involves a number of interlaced commitments: the conviction that the universe is ordered, not random; that there are truths that we do not invent but that we can come to know; that what we come to know and how we come to know it are not disparate matters; that faith and reason are companions, not enemies. This realism is critical, not credulous. We know that what we come to know is open to rethinking, to new insights, for we cannot know all there is to know in any scholarly field or in any dimension of human living-together. Critical realism knows there is a "there there." We do not just make things up and jerry-rig reality as we skip along life's post-everything pathway.

Yet another great advantage and strength of the Catholic tradition, as advanced through a commitment to critical realism within a capacious framework underscored by a sturdy anthropology, is the foregrounding of the dignified human person born *in communio*. Whether as mother or scientist, friend or philosopher, farmer or jurist, pacifist or soldier, our sociality goes all the way down even as our minds engage the worlds of which we are a part. What the world, and dominant ways of thinking about the world, drive apart—self/other; inner/outer; faith/reason; belief/criticism; family/society; arts/sciences—a "Catholic" approach draws together, yet at the same time helps to keep distinct. A distinction is different from the destructive divisions that so often pertain and that predictably throw out an unending series of false problems along the lines of: Do we start with individuals or with "society"? And what about the famous "one" and the "many"? Or "diverse" or "the same"? Posed in this way, and through these categories, we are always poised on the horns of unnecessary dilemmas. There are complexities enough in this world without making matters more difficult, even impossible to sort out, by consistently driving apart that which rightly belongs together—within a single frame—as distinctive, yet related. There is no "distinct" without some norm of "sameness"; no "one" without a "many"; no "individual" absent a "society."

Polkinghorne offers to the many nonscientists among us a recognition that science, too, has its variations on these themes. What prevailed in science for a long time was the insistence that complex phenomena could be isolated for scientific purposes, hived off, taken apart, and put back together again. This was part and parcel of a kind of Baconian "realism" that fragmented knowledge, by contrast to the richness of "the real." Working within the framework of a trinitarian theology, one is afforded a "pattern-forming agency": the world is a world of forms and the Trinity, as Augustine taught so brilliantly, is form-giving. Polkinghorne might describe this as reality's way of fighting back against atomistic reductionism. Trinitarian theism sets human powers within the most comprehensive possible version and vision of understanding: integration, once again, is the animating theme. How do we hold all this complexity together? How do we even come close to a world "endowed," as Polkinghorne so captivatingly put it, "with God's fertile intention"?

An Augustinian take on this, consistent with Polkinghorne's critical realism and Trinitarianism, would begin with the anthropological claim: being the sorts of creatures that we are, we see the world through forms or conceptual spectacles. As beings circumscribed by bounds of time and space, we require certain fundamental categories in order to apprehend the world at all. Form, which circumscribes, is also a presupposition of human freedom, necessary to our ability to reason things through. The primary form, for Augustine, is the form and form-giving category we call the Trinity, "a principle capable of saving the reason as well as the will, and thus redeeming human personality as a whole."[8] Immersed in time and space, with no possibility of escape, authentic knowledge should chasten and amaze us rather than inflate us. Polkinghorne conveys just such amazement as the reality of the world is disclosed slowly to human reason that has not shut the window to transcendence. Within this construal of God's relation to the world, God is not a meddler who pops in to intervene dramatically from time to time; rather, God continuously interacts with the world; the world is alive, quivering with intensities, awaiting our ongoing engagement with her.

That engagement will always be political, Bruce Russett reminds us. But must it be deadly? Are we fated to reenact a Hobbesian war of all against all until the eschaton? There are "realists" within the long tradition of politics, especially that branch called "international relations," who think so. Why? First, because there is no unifying, overarching power that can keep all the kingdoms contained, and second, because of the human propensity to pursue one's own individual or collective self-interest at the expense of that of another individual or collective. This framework, here roughly hewn, so prevails in the higher learning that it is akin to heresy to challenge it. But Catholic traditions not only do, they must. This challenge is not a total debunking, for Catholic thinkers in the "just war tradition," the most highly developed and continuous strand of Catholic thought where "the nations" and their wars are concerned, recognize not only the awful reality of war and violence, they see the occasional tragic necessity of resort to war and violence when a fundamental good is threatened or crushed. But violence is always put on trial, so to speak. Once again: critical realism.

In a system—a vast ecology of states, nations, and peoples encompassing the globe—in which the possibility of violence is always present, what integrative imperatives can be brought to bear? If the world is a world of sin—broken—it is also a world of order; it is not the chaos and "anarchy" so dear to the hearts of so many "IR" theorists, argues Russett. He reminds us that the way we depict or describe the world enters into and helps to bring that world into being because we may well foreclose certain possibilities—for greater comity and cooperation, for example—by declaring these imprudent or even impossible. In effect, Russett urges upon all scholars in international relations an approach that enables them to see the connections between various critical factors and features of the world such that they might be able to forestall a breakdown into violence before such becomes nigh inexorable. Russett calls his an "epidemiological perspective"—a variant on the ecological imperative, another way to see interactions and interconnections.

There is a fundamental starting assumption needed here, however, and it flies in the face of Hobbesian and Machiavellian insistencies, namely, that not everyone is a potential enemy; that there are structures of relationships, built up over time, that are sturdy. For example, we know that,

in case of disagreement between the United States and Great Britain, negotiation and compromise are in the offing. These two countries and cultures will not go to war against each other. The president of the United
States and the prime minister of Great Britain do not get out of bed every
morning and say, "What is my enemy in situ, the United States/United
Kingdom, up to today? What mask of friendship do we don today?" The
friendship is real. The two countries are not Hobbesian billiard balls that
are bound to collide sooner or later. Solidarity is a concept that is not
reserved to "domestic" politics, and hope is present that what Pope John
Paul II calls a "constructive logic of peace" might, over time, be built up
as a counterweight to the logic of war that has for too long pertained.

The logic of war flows, in our time, from the logic of state sovereignty,
enshrined at Westphalia in 1648, that holds that there is no "external"
right for one "state" to "intervene" in the affairs of another. Sovereignty is
a kind of solipsistic territoriality in this formulation. One state relates to
another the way porcupines are said to kiss. Internal to sovereign states,
there are those whose task is to serve that state: civil servants, they are
called. Nicholas Boyle offers a fascinating glimpse of arts and letters produced under the aegis of states (Germany) in a situation in which the pro-
fessoriate was formed as part of a wider intelligentsia whose raison d'être
was loyalty and service to the state. Theology was one such enterprise. In
a way, one might call this "bad integration," alerting us to the fact that
"integration" must be evaluated, for the terms under which phenomena
are integrated may militate against the vitality, freedom, and truths of
faith. The result of this integration in Germany was disastrous in practice, Boyle implies, as state dependence led to a reconciled (as in com-
promised) clergy who were weakened in relation to that state power they
were designed to serve.

Matters grow heavier as one views the triumph of an idealist epistemology with its tendency to make of art a kind of secularized religion
driven by an implicit pantheism. Art becomes rarified and precious, an
idealist "holy of holies." Boyle notes that aesthetics was, quite disastrously,
assigned an integrative task. The incarnational-Trinitarian worldview, the
dominant strand of Western literary realism with its emphasis on the concrete, the particular, and the possibility of a world redeemed and sancti-
fied through suffering, is not only abandoned, it is assaulted. Hans Urs
von Balthasar, according to Boyle, imposed that idealist aesthetics on
Catholic theology.

Fittingly, given the passing of the twentieth century, this volume ends with the post–World War II attempt to prevent any such horror from overtaking the West in particular, humanity in general, ever again. The name given to this ongoing effort is, of course, human rights. Mary Ann Glendon details the influence of Catholic natural law teaching (especially through the figure of the French philosopher, Jacques Maritain, and of the Lebanese Orthodox thinker, Charles Malik) on the Universal Declaration of Human Rights. The declaration serves as a potent example of what an integrated commitment to human dignity, freedom, and justice yields by way of offering up a framework that is universal in its claims and scope but particular in its application. Countering current prejudices against "universal" anything, Glendon argues that universal is not synonymous with "homogeneous." Further, a commitment to pluralism does not put one on a slippery slope to relativism. The Catholic tradition has long espoused a kind of loose-fitting universalism, cognizant of plural cultures and the differing capacities of diverse peoples in a mix of times and places to enact and embody universal truths and commitments.

Beginning with an integrated view of the human person, the Catholic tradition of human rights speaks to and of persons in their fullness as creatures who seek standing, freedom, and justice. This involves capacities and needs that every society should respect and find ways to make provision for. The implication for human rights is that societies are not permitted—normatively speaking—to pick and choose from among rights and say, in effect, "Okay, now. We'll stop torturing people. But they cannot worship openly and freely. We'll make sure they learn to read and to write. But you can forget about medical care." If one begins with an integrated person and places that person within a dense social ecology, the implications for human rights are made potently exigent.

Here it must be said that the Catholic tradition can sustain a commitment to human rights as an integrated endeavor of persons in community in a way that the dominant individualist-rights tradition of North American culture cannot. How so? Because Catholic social teaching puts together anthropological presuppositions, a concept of rights as social, and a vision of the goods toward which rights tend. Each right also names an obligation. This, too, is a form of integration, then, as rights are not in one category, duties and obligations in another. If there were two categories, then, as a second-order activity, one might go on to figure out what they have to do with each other. Catholic teaching, by contrast, puts them together as two sides of a coin. Obviously, none of this sorts out in any concrete case how the universal rights commitment is to be embodied and enacted in the Sudan or in South Carolina, in Pakistan or Pennsylvania. But it affords a powerful set of concepts, an epistemology (critical realism), and an animating framework.

After considering all this, one wants simply to say: let's roll up our sleeves, there's work to be done. As this volume displays so richly, Catholic traditions not only go hand in hand with higher learning, they helped to constitute the notion of the *universitas* in the first instance. If the university and Catholic traditions have fractured, divided, even been at war at moments in the past, a period of fruitful engagement now lies before us. I've always been rather inordinately fond of a line Robert Bolt puts in the mouth of St. Thomas More in his play *A Man for All Seasons*, when he gives More some wonderful words to speak to More's daughter, Meg: "God made the angels to show him splendor—as he made animals for innocence and plants for their simplicity. But Man he made to serve him wittily, in the tangle of his mind!"[9]

Wittily and well, turning our powers of discernment to the discovery of truths that serve the dignity of persons, that amaze us with the complexity of creation, that sometimes discomfit, sometimes soothe, that honor creature and Creator alike. The "ardent secularist" foil with which I began is called into service one more time at my conclusion: to such a secularist, faith is a way to put the mind to sleep, to stop the synapses from firing, to retreat into a cocoon of lulling fairytales. This volume alerts us to the restless, engaged energy and perspicuity that faith helps to make possible within, and for, the higher learning—to the benefit of all of us, teachers and learners committed, as we are pledged to be, to be the unearthers and guardians of truth.

NOTES

1. I put scare quotes round "secularist" just to signal the problematic nature of this category. We are all, in some sense, secularists, living in a "disenchanted" world, as it has been called. That is, we live in a world in which the category "religion" is often set up as a species of organization within a wider "secular" world. Or, "religion" may be construed as a foe of the "secular" or as battling over turf. Given the extraordinary success of modern sciences and the recognition of just how much "nature" has yielded her secrets to science in and through modes of rational analysis and experimentation that all but the most

rigidly antimodern accept, it is easy to understand how secular reason triumphed in so many spheres. Even so, the secular/religion divide is no longer particularly helpful. But we are stuck with it, as no workable substitutes have, to my knowledge, been proffered.

2. The film was released in 1960 and earned an Academy Award nomination for the great Spencer Tracy for best actor, though the award that year went to Burt Lancaster for "Elmer Gantry," a potent representation of a huckster evangelist: a real Hollywood v. the bumpkins bumper-crop year. Tracy played a character like Clarence Darrow, best known for saving killers Leopold and Loeb from the gas chamber and for his general opposition to the death penalty and all-purpose contribution to progressive causes. Both films, *Inherit the Wind* and *Elmer Gantry*, are terrific and both traffic in egregious stereotypes. We don't live in a perfect world.

3. This complexity is amply on display in the most recent of so many remarkable encyclicals issued by Pope John Paul II. I refer to *Fides et Ratio*, 1999.

4. Of course, I know about "Galileo and all that"—though even there, matters were more complex than they are usually represented—and that matter was long ago put to rest in practice and was officially put to rest under Pope John Paul II.

5. The reader should keep in mind that the essays in this volume were written in the context of the debate in the United States concerning the reception of *Ex corde ecclesiae* and the enormous controversy surrounding this document. I make no attempt here to adjudicate that controversy on my own; nor do I try to place the distinguished essays in this volume along a spectrum of embrace of the *Ex corde* imperative, or dissent—whether mild or militant—from it.

6. This does not, of course, mean that neo-Aristotelian Thomism simply has the field to itself. Rather, among this volume's contributors, MacIntyre made it his task to offer up an integrative desideratum in the fullest way. I conclude this chapter with a "building from the ground up" integrative imperative that starts with the human person.

7. Wolfe raises questions about the reliability of Putnam's data. I, for one, am convinced that Putnam's data point to complex truths about our current fragmentation.

8. This quotation is from Charles Norris Cochrane's classic, *Christianity and Classical Culture* (New York: Galaxy, 1959), 384. Augustine's *The Trinity* (Washington, D.C.: Catholic University of America Press, 1992), is the text in question.

9. Robert Bolt, *A Man for All Seasons* (New York: Vintage, 1960), 126.

Contributors

ALASDAIR MACINTYRE, Research Professor of Philosophy, University of Notre Dame, is the author of *A Short History of Ethics*, *After Virtue*, and *Dependent Rational Animals*.

ALAN WOLFE is a professor of political science and Director of the Center for Religion and American Public Life at Boston College. He is the author or editor of more than ten books, including *Marginalized in the Middle* and *One Nation, After All*. A contributing editor of *The New Republic* and *The Wilson Quarterly*, Professor Wolfe writes often for those publications as well as for *Commonweal*, *The New York Times*, *Harper's*, *The Atlantic Monthly*, *The Washington Post*, and other magazines and newspapers.

JOHN POLKINGHORNE was a theoretical elementary particle physicist and Professor of Mathematical Physics at Cambridge University, 1968–79. He was ordained an Anglican priest in 1982 and in 1996 retired from being President of Queens' College, Cambridge. He is the author of many books on science and theology, including *The Faith of a Physicist* and *Belief in God in an Age of Science*. He became a Fellow of the Royal Society in 1974 and was knighted by the Queen in 1997.

BRUCE RUSSETT is Dean Acheson Professor of International Relations and Political Science and Director of United Nations Studies at Yale. Since 1973 he has been editor of the *Journal of Conflict Resolution*. He was principal advisor to the U.S. Catholic Conference in writing their pastoral letter *The Challenge of Peace* in 1983. The most recent of his twenty-two books are *The Once and Future Security Council* and *Triangulating Peace: Democracy, Interdependence, and International Organizations* (forthcoming January 2001, with John R. Oneal).

NICHOLAS BOYLE is Head of the Department of German and Professor in German Literary and Intellectual History at Cambridge University. His publications include *Goethe. Faust Part One* (1987), *Goethe. The Poet and the Age* (volume 1,

1991; volume 2, 2000), and *Who Are We Now? Christian Humanism and the Global Market from Hegel to Heaney* (1998). In 1992 he received the Heinemann Prize of the Royal Society of Literature for *Goethe,* volume 1, and in 2000 he was awarded the Goethe Medal.

MARY ANN GLENDON is the Learned Hand Professor of Law at Harvard University. She teaches and writes in the fields of human rights, legal theory and international legal studies. Her books include *Rights Talk, A Nation Under Lawyers,* and the forthcoming *Rights from Wrongs,* a history of the framing of the Universal Declaration of Human Rights.

JEAN BETHKE ELSHTAIN is the Laura Spelman Rockefeller Professor of Social and Political Ethics at The University of Chicago. Among her books are *Democracy on Trial, Real Politics. Political Theory and Everyday Life, New Wine in Old Bottles. Politics and Ethical Discourse,* and *Where Are We? Critical Reflections and Hopeful Possibilities. Politics and Ethical Discourse.*

ROBERT E. SULLIVAN is Senior Associate Director of the Erasmus Institute and Associate Professor of History, University of Notre Dame.

Index